Macroeconomics

Instructor's Manual • Mark P. Moore
University of California - Irvine

SECOND EDITION

Macroeconomics

OLIVIER BLANCHARD

Prentice Hall, Upper Saddle River, NJ 07458

Acquisitions Editor: *Rod Banister*
Managing editor: *Gladys Soto*
Assistant editor: *Holly Jo Brown*
Project editor: *Theresa Festa*
Manufacturer: *Technical Communication Services*

Printed in the United States of America

10 9 8 7 6 5 4 3 2 1

ISBN 0-13-017268-5

Prentice-Hall International (UK) Limited, *London*
Prentice-Hall of Australia Pty. Limited, *Sydney*
Prentice-Hall Canada Inc., *Toronto*
Prentice-Hall Hispanoamericana, S.A., *Mexico*
Prentice-Hall of India Private Limited, *New Delhi*
Prentice-Hall of Japan, Inc., *Tokyo*
Prentice-Hall (Singapore) Pte Ltd
Editora Prentice-Hall do Brasil, Ltda., *Rio de Janeiro*

CONTENTS

Chapter 1. A Tour of the World

I. Motivating Question

What Is Macroeconomics?

The chapter does not provide an explicit or formal answer. Instead, it describes the issues of concern to macroeconomists who study the United States, Europe, and Asia. A working definition of macroeconomics at this point is the study of output, unemployment, and inflation, terms that will be defined precisely in Chapter 2.

II. Why the Answer Matters

This chapter attempts to provide students an incentive to master the theoretical material that follows in the remainder of the text. The implicit promise is that the theoretical model developed in the text will allow students to make sense of current economic problems of obvious importance around the world.

III. Key Tools, Concepts, and Assumptions

1. Tools and Concepts

Chapter 1 does not provide any analytical tools. However, it does force students to confront some basic data and introduces data sources for various regions of the world. In addition, the chapter introduces and defines briefly the concepts of output, growth, the unemployment rate, and the inflation rate. A precise definition of these terms follows in Chapter 2.

2. Assumptions

Implicit in the Tour of the World is the assumption that the same basic macroeconomic tools can be used to analyze economies throughout the world. It might be worth making this point explicitly. The macroeconomic framework developed in the text would be neither terribly useful, nor compelling as a theory, if it applied only to the United States, and not to the other market economies.

IV. Summary of the Material

1. Macroeconomic Performance of the United States

Following a recession (a period of negative output growth) ending in 1991, the United States has enjoyed an expansion (a period of positive output growth) since. At the time of this writing, the rates of unemployment and inflation are at relatively low levels, when compared to their average values since 1960. At the same time, the stock market is booming.

The issue is how long this combination of circumstances will last. Many economists believe that a continued low unemployment rate will ultimately create pressure on wages and prices and increase inflation—the growth of prices. If so, the Federal Reserve may decide to tighten monetary policy, which could lead to a recession. Likewise, if the stock market is overvalued, as some economists believe, a crash may create a recession.

Another area of concern is growing wage inequality. Beginning in the early 1980s and continuing through the mid-1990s, real wages (money wages adjusted for inflation) have grown much faster for some workers than for others. For example, real wages have increased by about one percent per year for workers with a college education, but decreased by about one percent per year for workers who have not finished high school. Some possible causes for growing wage inequality are sketched in this chapter and described more fully in Chapter 13.

Finally, even though the United States economy continues to grow, its average growth rate has fallen from 4.0% (for the period 1950-1973) to 2.6% (for the period 1974-1997).

2. Macroeconomic Performance of Europe

The countries of the European Union have together experienced positive but relatively low growth over the 1990s, combined with low inflation and continued high unemployment (relative to Europe in the 1960s and to the United States today). The debate over remedies for high unemployment is characterized by two polar views—the first argues for more activist monetary policy to stimulate output growth and the second for changes in labor market institutions to promote more flexibility in the labor market. At the same time, the European Union is in the midst of a grand experiment to form a single currency. Although this may reduce transactional inefficiencies associated with the use of separate national currencies, it will also eliminate the discretion of each country individually to use monetary policy to stimulate output and reduce unemployment. In the future, monetary policy will be conducted for all of Europe by a single group of policymakers, much in the way the United States Federal Reserve Board conducts monetary policy for all of the individual states of the United States.

3. Macroeconomic Performance of Asia

A number of Asian economies have achieved high growth, compared to the rest of the world, in the past thirty years. However, severe problems have emerged in the mid-1990s. In Japan, output growth has slowed substantially and the unemployment rate has reached record levels (for Japan). Many analysts attribute the poor economic performance to a collapse of stock market and real estate prices in the early 1990s. According to this argument, the decline in asset prices reduced the value of assets of Japanese banks and limited their ability to provide credit. Suitable remedies for poor economic performance are unclear. Expansionary fiscal and monetary policies have thus far had little effect.

In 1997, a number of other Asian economies suffered economic crises, characterized by rapid exchange rate depreciation, a steep fall in asset prices, and a fall in growth. In some cases, the reduction in growth was severe. Real GDP growth in Indonesia fell from 4.6% in 1997 to -13.7% in 1998 (Source: IMF *World Economic Outlook*, May 1999). Thailand, Malaysia, Korea, and Hong Kong also suffered deep recessions in 1998. Debate over the causes of the Asian crisis is framed by two extremes. One side blames the financial markets for speculative behavior; the other argues that financial markets were responding to economic problems resulting from fundamental policy errors—especially with regard to bank regulation—and corruption in Asian economies.

Finally, China has enjoyed rapid growth over the past twenty years, but remains poor on a per capita basis. Still, by virtue of its size, China is becoming one the main economic powers of the world.

V. Pedagogy

1. Points of Clarification

A subtle point that arises from the discussion of the macroeconomic data is the division of postwar time into pre- and post-1973. Since few of today's undergraduates would have been alive in 1973, a brief mention of the oil crisis (as well as the final collapse of the fixed-exchange rate system) would be helpful to introduce students to the seminal historical episodes of macroeconomics.

2. Alternative Sequencing

Output, the unemployment rate, and the inflation rate are not defined precisely until Chapter 2. Some instructors may prefer to cover the definitions from Chapter 2, and the discussion of why macroeconomists care about these variables, before discussing the material in this chapter.

3. Enlivening the Lecture

An alternative to posing the motivating question of this chapter is to ask students what they hope to learn from the course. The answers can be used to construct a description of what the course—and macroeconomics—is about. Likewise, rather than sticking to the facts presented in the chapter, one could ask students to raise questions about countries of interest to them.

Another alternative is to begin a lecture on this chapter (and the course) by asking whether the Fed should raise interest rates,[1] and to develop alternative opinions based on illustrative newspaper quotes or student answers. In addition to portraying macroeconomics as a lively and sometimes contentious field, this approach also immediately introduces students to the central issue of U.S. macroeconomic policy and connects the course with current topics in the news.

VI. Extensions

The Tour of the World presented in this chapter does not include developing countries outside Asia or the transition economies of Eastern Europe. Chapter 24 discusses the transition economies. For the developing economies, the continuing macroeconomic concerns are achieving lasting economic growth, alleviating poverty, and combining external adjustment with exchange rate stability. In principle, the World Bank addresses the first two of these issues, and the International Monetary Fund the third. Both institutions have come under criticism in recent years. The IMF, in particular, has been castigated by several prominent international economists for its handling of the Asian crisis. Chapter 24 describes the debate more fully.

Although not strictly an extension, instructors may wish to supplement the material in Chapter 1 with a review of the distinction between positive and normative economics, and a discussion of how normative perspectives can lead economists to different policy prescriptions even when they agree on the facts. Instructors may also wish to remind students of the difficulties that economists and other social scientists face because of the inability to conduct controlled experiments. A discussion of this sort was presented in Chapter 1 of the first edition of the text.

VII. Observations and Exercises

Average growth rates have fallen in the United States, Europe, and Japan. Perhaps this is more than coincidence. An open question is whether the fall in growth rates also applies to Asian economies other than Japan. Was the Asian crisis a temporary deviation from high growth rates, or will average growth rates in Asia be lower after the crisis than before?

---

[1] At the time of this writing (August 1999), the Fed had just implemented a widely anticipated increase in interest rates. Whether and how much the Fed would act to tighten monetary policy in the future was a point of debate.

Chapter 2. A Tour of the Book

I.   Motivating Questions

1. How Do Economists Define Output, the Unemployment Rate, and the Inflation Rate, and Why Do Economists Care about These Variables?

Output and the unemployment rate are defined in the usual fashion. Two alternative definitions of the inflation rate are presented: the percentage change in the GDP deflator and the percentage change in the CPI. The link between output and the standard of living is implicit in the chapter. Economists care about the unemployment rate because the unemployed suffer, particularly if they remain unemployed for long periods of time, and because the unemployment rate provides an indicator of whether the economy is growing too fast or too slowly (concepts that will be defined precisely later in the book).   Inflation has three main effects: it redistributes real income away from those who receive fixed nominal income, it distorts relative prices to the extent that some nominal variables do not adjust, and it creates uncertainty about relative price levels.

2. What Factors Affect Output in the Short Run, Medium Run, and Long Run?

This chapter introduces the basic framework of the book in terms of time. In the short run (a time frame of a few years), output is determined primarily by demand. In the medium run (a time frame of one or two decades), output is determined by the level of technology and the size of capital stock, both of which are more or less fixed. In the long run (a time frame of a half century or more), output is determined by technological progress and capital accumulation.

II. Why the Answer Matters

Students need a formal definition of the basic macroeconomic variables before they can proceed to analyze them. The discussion in this chapter provides enough information for students to begin looking at macroeconomic data in a rudimentary way. Moreover, some discussion of why economists care about these variables, particularly inflation, is useful to orient students. Without any discussion of the costs of inflation, for example, the current debate over whether unemployment is too low appears nonsensical.

III. Key Tools, Concepts, and Assumptions

1. Tools and Concepts

i. Chapter 2 introduces two general economic tools: **scatter diagrams** and **index numbers**.

ii. The chapter defines formally the basic macroeconomic concepts of **nominal** and **real GDP**, **GDP growth**, the **GDP deflator**, the **unemployment rate**, the **CPI**, and the **inflation rate**, as well as associated concepts such as **valued added**, **intermediate inputs**, the **labor force**, and the **participation rate**. All of these concepts are defined in the usual manner.

iii. Two empirical regularities—**Okun's Law** and the **Phillips Curve**—are introduced in the form of scatter diagrams. These empirical relationships link the three primary macroeconomic variables of output, the unemployment rate, and the inflation rate and establish the difficult choices facing policymakers in trying to reduce inflation or unemployment.

iv. The chapter distinguishes the **short run**, the **medium run**, and the **long run** in the manner described in part I. The distinction establishes the basic theoretical framework for the book.

IV. Summary of the Material

1. Aggregate Output

The text considers a closed economy until Chapter 18, so output is equated with GDP. Output has three equivalent definitions: (1) the value of final goods and services produced during a given period, (2) the sum of value-added during a given period, and (3) the sum of labor and capital income and indirect taxes.

Using the first definition, nominal GDP is output valued at current prices. Real GDP is output valued at constant prices. If the economy produced only one good—say, cars—and this good were unchanged over time, one could measure real GDP by simply counting the number of cars produced each year. Alternatively, one could multiply the number of cars by some constant price—say, the price in some base year. Thus, in the base year, real and nominal GDP would be the same. In practice, the construction of real GDP involves two complications. First, since the economy produces many goods, one must decide how to weight the value of output of each good to produce aggregate real GDP. The appendix to Chapter 2 discusses this issue in more detail. Second, the range of goods produced changes over time and the quality of similar goods changes over time. Economists who construct GDP try to account for quality change in goods through hedonic pricing, an econometric technique which estimates the market value of a good's characteristics—speed, durability, and so on.

The growth rate of real (nominal) GDP is the rate of change of real (nominal) GDP. Periods of positive GDP growth are called expansions; periods of negative growth, recessions.

2. Unemployment and Inflation

i. The Unemployment Rate and Okun's Law

An unemployed person is someone who does not have a job, but is looking for one. The labor force is the sum of those who have jobs, the employed, and the unemployed. The unemployment rate is the ratio of unemployed persons to the labor force. Those persons of working age who do not have a job and are not looking for one are classified as out of the labor force. The participation rate is the ratio of the labor force to the size of the working-age population.

Economists care about unemployment for two reasons. First, the unemployed suffer. Exactly how much depends on a number of factors, including the generosity of unemployment benefits and the duration of unemployment. In the United States, the average duration of unemployment is relatively low, but some groups (*e.g.*, ethnic minorities, the young, and the less skilled) tend to be more susceptible to unemployment and to remain unemployed much longer than average. Second, the unemployment rate helps policymakers assess how fast the economy should be growing. In most countries, there is a link between the growth rate of output and the change in the unemployment rate. When output growth is high, the unemployment rate decreases; when growth is low, the unemployment rate declines. This relationship—called Okun's law, after the economist who discovered it—offers policymakers some guide to how fast output should be growing. If policymakers believe that the unemployment rate is too high, they need to generate relatively high output growth to reduce it. If policymakers believe the unemployment rate is too low, they need to engineer relatively low output growth to increase unemployment. A more precise discussion of what constitutes an unemployment rate that is too high or too low is offered later in the book.

ii. The Inflation Rate and the Phillips Curve

The inflation rate is the growth rate of the aggregate price level. Since there are many goods produced and consumed in an economy, constructing the aggregate price level is not trivial. Macroeconomists use two primary measures of the aggregate price level. The first, the GDP deflator, is the ratio of nominal to real GDP. Since nominal and real GDP differ only because prices in any given year differ from the base year, the GDP deflator provides some measure of the average price level in the economy, relative to the base year. By construction, the GDP deflator is one in the base year. Since the choice of base year is arbitrary, the level of the GDP deflator is not well defined. The rate of change of the GDP deflator, however, is well defined. One measure of inflation is the rate of change of the GDP deflator. Measures with arbitrary levels but well-defined rates of change are called index numbers. The GDP deflator is an index number

An alternative measure of the price level is the Consumer Price Index—another index number. In the United States, this measure is based on price surveys across U.S. cities. The prices of various goods are weighted according to average consumer expenditure shares in the United States. The construction of the CPI and the construction of real GDP involve similar problems. One can also measure inflation as the rate of change in the CPI.

The relationship between inflation measured from the GDP deflator and inflation measured from the CPI is very close, but not perfect. Intuitively, since GDP is about production, the GDP deflator measures the average price of goods produced in a country. The CPI, on the other hand, attempts to measure the price of a representative basket of private consumption. Not all goods consumed are produced at home (some are imported from foreign countries), and not all goods produced at home are consumed by domestic households (some are consumed by the government, some by foreigners, and some by firms as intermediate goods).

Economists care about inflation because it can distort relative prices, produce uncertainty about relative prices, and redistribute income. Inflation distorts relative prices because some nominal variables (*e.g.*, tax brackets) do not immediately adjust to the rise in the aggregate price level. Inflation redistributes income because some transactions involve fixed nominal payments. For example, some retirees receive fixed nominal incomes (although the text notes that in the United States, the elderly have typically done better on average during inflationary periods). In addition, some loans (*e.g.*, standard mortgage loans) involve fixed nominal payments. When loan payments are nominally fixed, the real value of these payments falls with inflation, so borrowers gain and creditors lose.

There is an empirical relationship between the rates of inflation and unemployment. When the unemployment rate rises above a certain level, the inflation rate declines. When the unemployment rate falls below this level, the inflation rate increases. In the United States, this relationship, called the Phillips curve, has held since about 1970. The Phillips curve is the subject of Chapter 8.

3. The Basic Macroeconomic Framework and a Road Map for the Book

Macroeconomists view the economy in terms of three time frames. In the short run—a few years or so—demand for goods and services determines output. In the medium run—one or two decades—the level of technology and the size of the capital stock determine output. Since these variables change slowly, it is a useful simplification to assume that they are fixed in the medium run. Finally, in the long run, technological progress and capital accumulation are the primary determinants of output growth.

Chapters 3-13 are organized around these time frames. The remainder of the book presents extensions (expectations, the open economy) to the basic framework, analyzes episodes of unusually poor macroeconomic performance, and studies the scope for fiscal and monetary policy.

V. Pedagogy

1. Points of Clarification

The use of subscripts to index time will be new for many students. A few minutes of clarification may be worthwhile at the outset.

2. Alternative Sequencing

The chapter does not discuss national income accounting in any detail. Instead the relevant accounting identities are presented in the main text as they become relevant for the development of the analytical model. For example, Chapter 3 presents the expenditure side of the accounts in the course of explaining the composition of aggregate demand. A complete treatment of the national income and product accounts is also presented in Appendix 1. Instructors may prefer to introduce the material from Appendix 1 immediately after Section 1 of this chapter.

3. Enlivening the Lecture

It is difficult to add much life to the definitions chapter of macroeconomics. One way to reduce the number of definitions is to focus only on output at this point, and leave the unemployment and inflation definitions until Chapter 6, which introduces the labor market and aggregate supply. The benefit of this approach is a more rapid advance to the Keynesian cross in Chapter 3. The cost is the lack of discussion of the Phillips curve, which addresses a current policy issue, and the need to say something about the aggregate price level in the LM curve in Chapter 5.

VI. Extensions

1. GDP as a Measure of Welfare

The chapter discusses briefly why economists care about inflation and unemployment, but does not do the same for GDP. It is probably obvious that economists use GDP as a gross measure of aggregate welfare, but instructors may wish to point out that there are (at least) three limitations on GDP as a welfare measure:

    i. Measured GDP values goods and services at market prices, since these reflect the relative values placed on them by consumers. However, some valuable things are not sold on the market, and their values thus have to be imputed, a process that undoubtedly introduces some errors. Two important services that do not have a market price are government services and owner-occupied housing.

    ii. Some goods and services not traded in markets are omitted altogether from the GDP calculation. For example, the value of leisure and the value of services performed in the household are not included in GDP. From a broader perspective, one might also cite civil liberties and other political "goods" as nonmarket goods produced by a nation, but not included in GDP.

    iii. GDP does not account for the fact that some of a nation's wealth is depleted in the process of producing it. NDP corrects this to some extent by subtracting the value of depreciated physical capital, but depletion of natural and environmental resources is still omitted. The Department of

Commerce and others have experimented with adjustments to GDP to account for resource and environmental depletion, but there is no consensus among economists about the proper methodology.

2. *Stocks and Flows: Wealth and GDP*

The text does not introduce the concepts of stocks and flows until Chapter 4 (Financial Markets). Instructors could introduce these concepts in this chapter by distinguishing national wealth (a stock) from GDP (a flow). A natural definition of national wealth is the value of the nation's land (including natural resources), physical and human capital, and claims on foreigners at a given point in time.

VII. Observations

1. *Conceptual Observations*

The value of GDP on the expenditure side is identical to the value on the income side. In other words, aggregate spending is identical to aggregate income. Emphasizing this point to students in this chapter will prepare them for Chapter 3, in which Y plays two roles—the value of production and the income potentially receivable by households, who own the factors of production. Because Y plays two roles, it appears on the left-hand side and the right-hand side of the goods market equilibrium equation.

2. *Empirical Observations*

Between 1960 and 1997, the share of services (as opposed to goods) in U.S. nominal GDP increased from 39% to 54%. Some explanations of productivity slowdown and rising inequality in the United States emphasize the increase in the share of services. On the other hand, in terms of chained 1992 dollars, the share of services in GDP was about the same in 1960 (52%) as in 1997 (52%). The introduction of chained GDP has made some difference in this calculation. Under the old, base-year calculation, the real share of services in 1982 dollars was 45% in 1960 and 51% in 1993. Under the new, chained methodology, the figures are 52% in 1960 and 54% in 1993. Of course, the latter figures also reflect revisions to the raw GDP numbers. (Source: *Economic Report of the President*, 1995, 1999)

Chapter 3. The Goods Market

I. Motivating Question

How Is Output Determined in the Short Run?

Output is determined by equilibrium in the goods market, *i.e.*, by the condition that supply (production of goods) equals demand. This condition always determines output, but in the short run, we assume that supply of goods is perfectly price-elastic. Thus, in the short run, output is effectively determined by demand. Moreover, in this chapter, investment is characterized as independent of the interest rate, so there is no need to consider simultaneous equilibrium of goods and financial markets.

II. Why the Answer Matters

The determination of output is the basic issue confronting macroeconomics. This chapter introduces the topic through the Keynesian cross model, which considers the goods market in isolation. The Keynesian cross provides basic intuition about model building and solving, output determination, and the role of fiscal policy. The short-run, qualitative results generally survive in more complicated models. Chapter 4 examines the financial markets in isolation, and Chapter 5 combines the goods and financial markets to construct the demand side of the economy.

III. Key Tools, Concepts, and Assumptions

1. Tools and Concepts

i. The chapter introduces **functional notation**. An appendix discusses functions in more detail.

ii. The chapter introduces modeling terminology: **exogenous** and **endogenous variables, behavioral equations**, **identities**, and **equilibrium conditions**.

iii. The chapter describes the **Keynesian cross** model, and associated terms, such as the (marginal) **propensity to consume, disposable income**, and **autonomous expenditure**.

iv. The chapter introduces **fiscal policy**.

2. Assumptions

i. The text assumes that the economy produces a single good. This assumption is maintained throughout most of the formal work in the book.

ii. After introducing the national income identity, the text assumes a closed economy. This assumption is maintained until Chapter 18.

iii. For short-run analysis, the text assumes that production adjusts automatically to output without changes in price, *i.e.*, that the supply curve is perfectly price elastic. This assumption implies that the price level is fixed. Although the price level is not discussed in this chapter, it is worthwhile to clarify the fixed-price assumption before discussing the LM curve in Chapters 4 and 5. This assumption is maintained until Chapter 6.

iv. Within the short-run context, the critical assumption of this chapter is that investment does not respond to the interest rate. This isolates the goods market from the financial market. This assumption will be relaxed in Chapter 5.

v. The chapter, in fact, goes further, and assumes that investment is exogenous. It does not depend on output, nor is there inventory investment, either planned or unplanned. Chapter 5 introduces the dependence of investment on output. This chapter discusses in words dynamic implications of allowing unplanned inventory adjustment, although it does not stress the point.

IV. Summary of the Material

1. The Composition of GDP

On the expenditure side, GDP can be decomposed into consumption (C), government spending (G), fixed investment (I), net exports (X-Q), and inventory investment (I_s).

2. The Demand for Goods

Assume there is only one good, and use the decomposition of GDP to think about demand for that good. Assume the economy is closed, so that net exports are zero, and ignore inventory investment, which is typically a small part of GDP. Then demand (Z) can be written as

$$Z=C+I+G \tag{3.1}$$

Write consumption as a linear function of disposable income (Y_D), which is income minus taxes (T):

$$C=c_0+c_1(Y_D)= c_0+c_1(Y\text{-}T) \tag{3.2}$$

The parameter c_0, which represents how much consumption would occur even if disposable income were zero, is called autonomous consumption or consumer confidence. The parameter c_1, which represents the increase in consumption for every extra unit of disposable income, is called the (marginal) propensity to consume. Assume that households do not consume every dollar of additional income, but save some, so that $0 < c_i < 1$.

Assume that investment is exogenous, and call it $\bar{I}$. Assume that government spending and taxes are exogenous, and under the control of the fiscal authorities. Substitute for consumption and investment, and rewrite demand:

$$Z = c_0 + c_i(Y-T) + \bar{I} + G \tag{3.3}$$

3. The Determination of Equilibrium Output

Output is determined by equilibrium in the goods market. The equilibrium condition is that production equals demand. Assume for now that production simply increases or decreases with demand without any change in price. Formally, assume that production is infinitely elastic with respect to price. Thus, in the short run, output is fully determined by demand. Then, we can write the equilibrium condition, $Y=Z$, as

$$Y = c_0 + c_i(Y-T) + \bar{I} + G \tag{3.4}$$

The variable Y appears on both sides of this equation. On the LHS, Y represents production. On the RHS, Y represents national income. Chapter 2 explained why these two quantities are equal. The aim of this model is to determine Y, an endogenous variable. To solve the model, it is necessary to write Y as a function of the exogenous variables, *i.e.*, those determined outside the model.

$$Y = [1/(1- c_i)][c_0 - c_i T + \bar{I} + G] \tag{3.5}$$

Equation (3.5) shows the algebraic solution and Figure 3.1 the graphical solution. In the graph, equilibrium occurs where demand (the ZZ curve) crosses the 45° line (*i.e.*, the line along which $Y=Z$).

Equilibrium income is the product of two factors—autonomous spending (the second term in brackets in equation (3.5)) and a "multiplier" (the first term in brackets). Assume that autonomous spending is positive,[1] which (given that $c_i < 1$) will be true unless the budget surplus, T-G, is very large. The multiplier, which depends on the value of the propensity to consume, arises because consumption is affected by income. Suppose there is an increase in autonomous consumption—say, because of an increase in consumer confidence. The initial increase in consumption because of the rise in c_0 leads to an increase in income. The increase in income leads to a further increase in consumption, which leads to a further increase in income, and so on. Thus, the effect of the initial increase in consumer confidence is "multiplied." The multiplier captures this effect. The text describes a more formal way to think of the

---

[1] Note that this assumption implies that the ZZ curve intersects the vertical axis at a point greater than zero. The restriction that $c_i < 1$ implies that the ZZ curve intersects the 45° line.

13

multiplier as the limit of a geometric series of fractional increases in consumption. A box also suggests that a fall in consumer confidence was responsible for the 1991 recession.

Figure 3.1: Equilibrium in the Goods Market

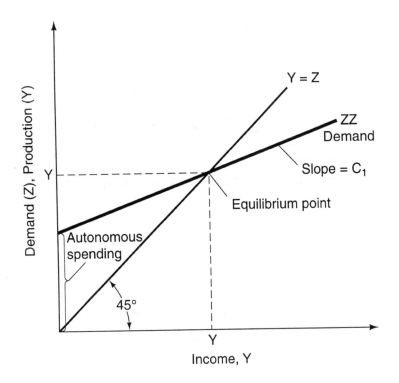

4. Investment Equals Saving: An Alternative Way of Thinking about Goods Market Equilibrium

Private saving is defined as disposable income minus consumption, or

$$S=Y-T-C \tag{3.6}$$

Using this definition, the equilibrium output condition ($Y=C+I+G$) can be expressed as:

$$I=S+(T-G) \tag{3.7}$$

In a closed economy, investment equals private (consumer) saving (S) plus government saving ($T-G$). The quantity $T-G$ is called the budget surplus. The quantity $G-T$ is called the budget deficit.

14

5. Is the Government Really Omnipotent? A Warning

The equilibrium output condition (3.5) seems to imply that the government, by choosing G and T, has absolute control over the level of output. The text stresses that this chapter provides only a first pass at the analysis of fiscal policy. Later chapters will make clear the many limitations on the ability of the government to control output through spending and taxation.

6. Appendix: An Introduction to Econometrics

Appendix 3 provides an informal introduction to ordinary least squares and instrumental variables and estimates the marginal propensity to consume with each method.

V. Pedagogy

1. Points of Clarification

i. In ordinary language, the term investment is commonly used to indicate the purchase of a financial asset. In macroeconomics, "investment" typically refers to fixed investment, defined as the purchase of newly produced physical capital. Moreover, "investment" typically is understood to include only fixed investment by firms, and not residential fixed investment—the purchase of new houses by households.

ii. The chapter assumes that the economy produces only one item and calls this item a "good." However, the model is not meant to be limited to physical goods as opposed to services. "Goods" is often used to refer to both physical goods and services.

2. Alternative Sequencing

For simplicity, investment is taken as exogenous. Chapter 5 describes the effects of output and the interest rate on investment in the course of developing the IS-LM model. An alternative would be to introduce the dependence of investment on the interest rate in this chapter, and then assume a fixed interest rate. Since assuming a fixed interest rate is essentially equivalent to assuming exogenous investment, this approach removes an (arguably) unnecessary step in the development of the IS-LM framework. It also allows for early experiments with the effects of changes in the interest rate on output as a precursor to the derivation of the IS curve. On the other hand, introducing the interest rate at this stage complicates the simple Keynesian cross story.

One could go further and introduce the dependence of investment on output as well. Conceptually, this step may be a bit too much for students in their first exposure to the Keynesian cross. At the very least, it seems wise to start with the effect of the interest rate on investment, and then add the effect of output.

3. Enlivening the Lecture

The chapter does not explicitly cover fiscal policy experiments. Explaining these in lecture reinforces concepts and provides an opportunity to link the model to current policy debates. For example, instructors could take a first pass at the likely effects of a tax cut to return part of the federal budget surplus to households. Depending upon the state of the economy, the tax cut could easily be adopted as a recurring theme for the course. The response of the Federal Reserve could be incorporated in Chapter 6, which develops IS-LM; the effects of the response on unemployment in Chapter 7, which develops AD-AS; and the motivation for the response in Chapter 8, on the Phillips curve. In general, instructors should bear in mind how quickly policy examples become dated for relatively young undergraduate students.

VI. Extensions

1. Macroeconomic Models

Some instructors may wish to supplement the discussion of model building in the text by distinguishing a model's structural form from its reduced form and by explaining the requirement that the number of equations equal the number of exogenous variables. A model's structural form sets out the model's postulates about behavior, definitions, and equilibrium conditions. A model's reduced form expresses the endogenous variables in terms of the exogenous ones. The number of equations must equal the number of unknowns if the model is to provide a complete (not underdetermined) and coherent (not overdetermined) explanation of the phenomenon of interest.

2. Inventory Investment

As noted in part III, apart from a few words in the text, the formal model of this chapter abstracts from inventory investment. This simplifies the presentation and allows the identification of aggregate demand with final sales. As an alternative, instructors could introduce and distinguish desired and undesired inventory investment and characterize goods-market equilibrium by the condition that unintended inventory investment equals zero. In this approach, aggregate demand does not, in general, equal final sales.

3. Fiscal Policy

The discussion in the text omits several familiar fiscal policy issues, including the balanced-budget multiplier, the role of income taxes, and the full-employment surplus as an indicator of fiscal policy.

The balanced-budget multiplier result helps illustrate the multiplier concept. The immediate effect of an increase in G is to increase output by the same amount. If taxes are increased by the same amount as G, however, there is no effect on disposable income (Y-T), and hence no effect on consumption. So the multiplier process aborts after the initial effect on output. In other words, the balanced-budget multiplier is one.

The introduction of income taxes, say, by defining T as $T=t_0+t_1Y$, implies a revision of the multiplier (to $1/[1-c_1(1-t_1)]$), and thus reinforces the notion that the multiplier is not a constant of nature, but depends on the structure of the model. In addition, the introduction of income taxes highlights the role of the federal budget as an automatic stabilizer, and leads naturally to an early discussion of the macroeconomic effects of a balanced-budget amendment to the United State Constitution. Finally, by demonstrating that the government budget has an endogenous component, the addition of income taxes to the model raises questions about the use of the fiscal surplus as an indicator of fiscal policy.

The latter point motivates discussion of the full-employment surplus as an alternative indicator of fiscal policy. The full-employment surplus improves upon the ordinary fiscal surplus by attempting to account for cyclical components of the government budget. However, the full-employment surplus has its own limitations; for example, it fails to reflect the differing effects of spending and taxation on autonomous expenditure.

VII. Observations

1. Conceptual Observations

i. Government spending includes the purchase of newly produced goods and services, not total government outlays. In particular, transfers—such as Social Security payments, veterans' benefits, and interest on the government debt—are excluded. Note also that government spending includes spending by all levels of government (federal, state, and local) and that some government spending pays for capital goods. Likewise, taxes are also net of transfers and include taxes collected at all levels of government.

ii. Imports are subtracted from GDP on the expenditure side because the spending categories comprise all spending, including spending on foreign goods and services. To isolate spending on domestically-produced goods and services, imports must be subtracted. Likewise, exports are added because they represent foreign spending on domestically produced goods and services.

2. Empirical Observations

Consumption typically accounts for about two-thirds of nominal GDP (68% in 1997).

Chapter 4. Financial Markets

I. Motivating Question

How Is the Interest Rate Determined in the Short Run?

The interest rate is determined by equilibrium in the money market, *i.e.*, by the condition that money supply equals money demand. Since the text abstracts from all assets other than bonds and money, equilibrium in the money market is equivalent to equilibrium in the bond market. In this chapter, nominal income is taken as given, so there is no need to consider simultaneous equilibrium of goods and financial markets.

II. Why the Answer Matters

Investment is a function of the interest rate (as will be discussed in Chapter 5), so output is affected by the interest rate. In addition, the determination of the interest rate is intimately connected with monetary policy. This chapter takes nominal GDP, which affects money demand, as given, so the financial markets can be considered in isolation from the goods market. Chapter 5 will address the joint determination of output and the interest rate in the short run.

III. Key Tools, Concepts, and Assumptions

1. Tools and Concepts

i. The chapter defines **stock** and **flow** variables and distinguishes wealth (a stock) from income (a flow).

ii. The chapter introduces **monetary policy** and describes **open market operations**.

iii. The chapter makes use of **balance sheets** for the central bank and private banks.

iv. The chapter introduces various terms and concepts associated with the banking system. These include **currency**, **checkable deposits**, **reserves**, **central bank money (high-powered money**, the **monetary base)**, and the **money multiplier**.

2. Assumptions

i. This chapter assumes that nominal GDP is given. More precisely, the chapter maintains the fixed-price level assumption from Chapter 3 and adds the assumption that real income is given. Chapter 5 considers the joint determination of the interest rate and real income.

ii. For clarity, the chapter assumes that money and bonds are the only assets available and that money does not pay interest. Money is divided into currency and checkable deposits in the section of the chapter that describes the banking system. Apart from a few words and exercises, the assumption that money does not pay interest is maintained throughout the book. Later chapters introduce other financial assets—stocks and bonds of different maturities—and physical capital.

IV. Summary of the Material

1. Money versus Bonds

Suppose the financial markets include only two assets—money, which can be used to purchase goods and services and pays no interest, and bonds, which cannot be used for transactions, but pay a positive interest rate *i*. Financial wealth equals the sum of money and bonds.

Financial wealth is a stock variable, *i.e.*, a variable whose value can be measured at any point in time. An individual's financial wealth changes over time by saving or dissaving, but at any given moment, financial wealth is fixed. Saving is a flow variable, *i.e.*, a variable whose value is meaningful only when expressed in terms of a time period. Income is also a flow variable. One speaks of income per year or income per month.

At every moment, households must decide how to allocate their given financial wealth between money and bonds. Since financial wealth is fixed, once the demand for money is known, so is the demand for bonds, and vice-versa. Accordingly, the chapter restricts attention to the demand for money.

By assumption, money is needed for transactions. Although it is hard to measure the overall level of transactions in the economy, it seems reasonable to assume that the level of transactions is proportional to nominal income, denoted $Y. So, money demand should be proportional to $Y. On the other hand, allocating wealth to money comes at the cost of forgone interest on bonds. So, money demand should decrease with the interest rate. Putting these observations together, the chapter specifies money demand as

$$M^d = \$YL(i) \tag{4.1}$$

where the function *L* decreases as the interest rate increases.

2. The Determination of the Interest Rate I

Assume all money is currency, so there are no checking accounts or banks. Consider the supply of money to be fully in the control of the central bank and take nominal income as given. Then, equilibrium in the money market occurs when the supply of money (M) equals the demand for money (M^d) given in equation (4.1). Figure 4.1 illustrates the solution.

3. Enlivening the Lecture

Casual empiricism suggests that undergraduates have more immediate interest in material related to financial markets than in material related to output, inflation, and unemployment, particularly when the United States has very little inflation or unemployment. A discussion relating the material of the chapter to current Federal Reserve policy (perhaps with a few words about the stock market's response to Fed policy) would probably be interesting to students.

Another suggestion is to look at the interest rate section of the financial pages of a major newspaper during the lecture. Besides making the financial pages a bit more accessible to students, this strategy might also provide an opportunity to discuss the inverse relationship between prices and interest rates. This relationship is discussed in the text.

VI. Extensions

1. The Balance Sheet Constraint

To clarify the relationship between bond market and money market equilibrium, it may be useful to be more explicit about the implications of the balance sheet constraint. The constraint implies

$$M^d + B^d = Financial\ Wealth = M + B, \text{ or}$$

$$(M^d - M) = (B - B^d)$$

In other words, the excess demand for money must equal the excess supply of bonds. When one market clears, the other must clear as well.

2. The Money Demand Function

This chapter assumes a money demand function of the form $M^d = \$YL(i) = PYL(i)$. A more general alternative would be $M^d = L(\$Y, i)$. The functional form assumed in the chapter allows for an easy conversion to real money demand by dividing through by the price level. Introducing the more general form requires explaining to students that money demand should be homogeneous of degree one in P. On the other hand, this exercise does make clear what is assumed, and reinforces understanding of a basic practice of economics, namely, the selection of convenient functional forms.

VII. Observations

1. Conceptual Observations

i. The chapter discusses the portfolio decisions of the nonbank public. The supply of money refers to the amount of money held by the nonbank public (not the government, the Federal Reserve, or banks).

ii. Money demand refers to a portfolio decision, the amount of fixed wealth that the nonbank public desires to hold in money as opposed to bonds. Money demand does not refer to the demand for income or wealth.

iii. The Federal Reserve does not create bonds, only money. It conducts open market operations with government bonds. The stock of government bonds outstanding is the government (in popular usage, national) debt, which is the product of past fiscal deficits. Open market operations apportion this debt between the Federal Reserve and the private sector.

2. Empirical Observations

i. The text notes that the ratio of M1 to nominal GDP fell from 27% in 1960 to 13% in 1997. Over the same time period, the ratio of M2 to nominal GDP also fell (from 59% to 50%), but the ratio of M3 to nominal GDP rose (from 60% to 66%). The monetary aggregates are mentioned in this chapter and discussed in more detail in Chapter 26.

ii. As noted in the text, the Federal Reserve can set the required reserve ratio between 7% and 22%. The actual reserve ratio is about 10 percent.

iii. In July 1999, currency accounted for about 44% of M1. (Source: Federal Reserve Release H.6) Coupled with a reserve ratio of 10%, this implies a money multiplier of about 2.

Chapter 5. Goods and Financial Markets: The IS-LM

I. Motivating Question

How Are Output and the Interest Rate Simultaneously Determined in the Short Run?

Output and the interest rate are determined by simultaneous equilibrium in the goods and money markets. In the short run, we assume that supply is infinitely elastic with respect to price (*i.e.*, price is fixed), so output is determined by demand.

II. Why the Answer Matters

The determination of output is the fundamental issue in macroeconomics. The interest rate affects output (through investment) and output affects the interest rate (through money demand), so it is necessary to consider the simultaneous determination of output and the interest rate.

III. Key Tools, Concepts, and Assumptions

1. Tools and Concepts

i. The chapter introduces the **IS-LM** framework.

ii. The chapter introduces the option of choosing alternative **policy mixes** to achieve macroeconomic goals.

iii. The chapter introduces the use of "+" and "-" above (or below) the arguments of a function to indicate the effect of an increase in the value of the argument on the value of the function.

2. Assumptions

i. This chapter maintains the fixed-price assumptions of previous chapters, but relaxes the assumptions that investment is independent of the interest rate (assumed in Chapter 3) and that nominal income is fixed (assumed in Chapter 4). Investment is also allowed to depend on output. The point of this chapter is to show how goods and financial markets are related and, thus, how output and the interest rate are simultaneously determined.

ii. The chapter continues to assume that inventory investment is zero and that the economy is closed.

IV. Summary of the Material

1. The Goods Market and the IS Relation

First, relax the assumption that investment is endogenous. In terms of the framework developed thus far, investment should depend on two factors: sales and the interest rate. A firm facing an increase in sales will need to purchase new plant, equipment, or both to increase production. Thus, investment increases when sales increase. An increase in the interest rate will increase the cost of borrowing needed to purchase new plant and equipment. Thus, investment decreases when the interest rate increases. These points describe an investment function of the following form:

$$I = I(\overset{+}{Y}, \overset{-}{i}) \tag{5.1}$$

Although the discussion suggests that investment should depend on sales, rather than income, the chapter continues to assume that inventory investment is zero, so income equals sales.

With the revised investment function, the closed-economy, goods-market equilibrium condition becomes

$$Y = C(Y-T) + I(Y,i) + G \tag{5.2}$$

For a fixed interest rate, the Keynesian cross analysis of Chapter 3 holds with two caveats. First, demand for goods and services (the RHS of equation (5.2)) is no longer assumed to be linear. Second, an additional assumption is required to ensure an equilibrium (*i.e.*, that the ZZ curve intersects the 45° - line). A sufficient assumption for this purpose is that the sum of the (marginal) propensity to consume out of income and the (marginal) propensity to invest out of income is less than one.

Equation (5.2) is called the IS relation, because (as shown in Chapter 3) goods-market equilibrium is equivalent to the condition that investment equals saving. To trace out an IS curve, start with a Keynesian cross with a given interest rate, then vary the interest rate. A decrease in the interest rate increases the level of investment for any level of output, and thus shifts the ZZ curve up. So output increases. Thus, the IS curve has a negative slope in *Y-i* space (Figure 5.1).

2. Financial Markets and the LM Relation

Start with the money-market equilibrium condition from Chapter 4, rewrite nominal income as *PY* (where P is the price level), and divide by *P* to derive the condition in real terms:

$$M/P = YL(i) \tag{5.3}$$

Real money market equilibrium is characterized by the same graph developed in Chapter 4, but the real money supply (*M/P*) is substituted for the nominal money supply (*M*). The chapter maintains the short-run assumption of a fixed price and, abstracting from details of monetary policy, assumes that *M* is under the control of the central bank.

Equation (5.3) is called the LM (Liquidity-Money) relation. To graph it in *Y-i* space, start with the money-market equilibrium graph and vary *Y*. Chapter 4 demonstrated that an increase in nominal income would increase the interest rate. Since the price is fixed, clearly an increase in real income will have the same effect. Thus, the LM curve has a positive slope in *Y-i* space (Figure 5.1).

3. *The IS-LM Model: Exercises*

The equilibrium values of *i* and *Y* are those that simultaneously satisfy the goods-market equilibrium condition (5.2) and the money-market equilibrium condition (5.3). Graphically, these values are determined by the point of intersection of IS and LM as illustrated in Figure 5.1.

Figure 5.1: The IS-LM Model

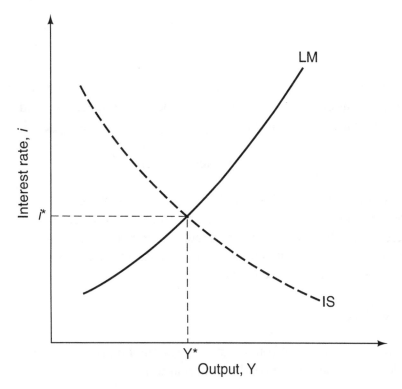

Changes in the equilibrium values of output and the interest rate (*Y** and *i**) can be brought about only as the result of shifts in the IS curve, the LM curve, or both. An increase in the money supply, which shifts the LM curve to the right, increases equilibrium output and reduces the equilibrium interest rate. An increase in taxes (or a reduction in government spending), which shifts the IS curve to the left, reduces equilibrium output and reduces the equilibrium interest rate. The text notes that an increase in taxes will have an ambiguous effect on investment, since the output effect tends to reduce investment, but the interest rate effect tends to increase it. More generally, although deficit reduction increases public (government) saving, it does not necessarily increase investment, because private saving is endogenous.

4. Using a Policy Mix

The text considers the consequences of combinations of fiscal and monetary policy through two examples. The deficit reduction during President Clinton's first term provides an example of contractionary fiscal policy coupled with expansionary monetary policy. German reunification offers an example of expansionary fiscal policy coupled with contractionary monetary policy.

5. Adding Dynamics

To introduce dynamics, the text assumes that the financial market adjusts to disturbances much more rapidly than the goods market. More precisely, the text assumes that the economy always operates on the LM curve, but may operate off of the IS curve during the adjustment to equilibrium. Thus, if there is a shift of the IS curve (but no shift of the LM curve), the economy will move gradually along the LM curve from its initial equilibrium to its new equilibrium. If there is a shift of the LM curve (but no shift of the IS curve), the interest rate will immediately jump to the new LM curve. Over time, the economy will travel along the new LM curve to its new equilibrium. The latter analysis implies that a change in monetary policy (or any shift of the LM curve) will cause the interest rate to overshoot its final equilibrium. The chapter notes this point, without using the term overshooting. This term will be introduced in Chapter 21, which discusses exchange rates.

6. Does the IS-LM Model Actually Capture What Happens in the Economy?

As evidence of the empirical relevance of the IS-LM model, the text describes the results presented in Christiano, Eichenbaum, and Evans, "The Effects of Monetary Policy Shocks: Evidence From the Flow of Funds," *Review of Economics and Statistics*, February 1996. The paper describes the dynamic responses of several important macroeconomic variables to a one percent increase in the Federal Funds rate.

V. Pedagogy

1. Points of Clarification

It is easy for trained economists to overlook the subtlety of the IS-LM model. Undergraduates who study intermediate macroeconomics are typically just coming to terms with the notion of equilibrium in one market, let alone simultaneous equilibrium in two markets. Two general points deserve repeated discussion.

First, the derivation of the IS and LM curves will take time for students to understand. It is important to emphasize that each point on the IS curve represents an equilibrium in the goods market and each point on the LM curve represents an equilibrium in the money market. In other words, the level of Y on the IS curve associated with any given interest rate is given by the intersection of the Keynesian cross for that interest rate. Likewise the value of i on the LM curve associated with any given level of output is given by the intersection of (real) money demand and (real) money supply in the money market equilibrium diagram.

Second, students may wonder why an increase in the interest rate does not shift the LM curve, since the interest rate affects money demand, or the IS curve, since the interest rate affects investment. It is worthwhile to emphasize that variables that appear on the axes of a diagram cannot shift the curves in the diagram. Only variables that do not appear on the axes can shift the curves. Moreover, in the case of IS-LM, the variables on the axes are the endogenous variables. Changes in exogenous variables or parameters shift the IS and LM curves.

VI. Extensions

1. Behavioral Parameters, the Slopes of the IS and LM Curves, and Policy Effectiveness

The text does not discuss the slopes of the IS and LM curves and the influence of behavioral parameters on the effectiveness of policy. With respect to the slopes, the more sensitive money demand is to income relative to the interest rate, the steeper the LM curve. Likewise, the more sensitive goods demand ($C+I+G$) is to income relative to the interest rate (through investment), the steeper the IS curve.

On the effectiveness of policy, there are two options to bring out the basic points. The first is to choose a simple linear specification and work out the relationship between the output effect of policy and behavioral parameters. A second option is to discuss the issue more heuristically. For example, consider an increase in government spending, and proceed in three steps.

i. For any given interest rate, the effect of fiscal policy on output will depend on the multiplier, modified to include endogenous investment. The larger the multiplier, *i.e.*, the greater the sensitivity of consumption and investment to output, the larger the initial response of output.

ii. Since an increase in G will increase Y, it will also increase the quantity of money demanded for any interest rate, and thus increase the interest rate, in order to maintain money market equilibrium. The increase in the interest rate will be small to the extent that money demand is not very sensitive to income, but is very sensitive to the interest rate. If money demand is not very sensitive to income, then the excess demand for money created by the increase in G will be small. If money demand is very sensitive to the interest rate, the increase in the interest rate needed to restore equilibrium in the money market will be small.

iii. Finally, the increase in the interest rate will tend to reduce investment and thus offset some of the initial increase in output. This effect will be small to the extent that investment is not very sensitive to the interest rate.

In sum, fiscal policy will have a greater effect on output to the extent that the multiplier is large, money demand is not very sensitive to income, money demand is very sensitive to the interest rate, and investment is not very sensitive to the interest rate.

One could carry out the same exercise with respect to monetary policy. An increase in the money supply affects output by reducing the interest rate and increasing investment. Thus, an increase in the money supply will tend to have a large effect on output when it has a large effect on the interest rate, which will be true when money demand is not very sensitive to the interest rate. The interest rate will have a large effect on output when investment is very sensitive to the interest rate, which calls forth the initial response of output, and, again, when the multiplier is large. The increase in output increases the quantity of money demanded for any interest rate, and tends to increase the interest rate, offsetting some of the initial effect of the increase in the money supply. This effect will be small when the demand for money is not very sensitive to income.

In sum, monetary policy will have a greater effect on output to the extent that money demand is not very sensitive to the interest rate, investment is very sensitive to the interest rate, the multiplier is large, and money demand is not very sensitive to income.

These exercises are relatively sophisticated, but they make clear the linkages between the goods market and the money market through the interest rate.

2. Interest Rate Targeting

Throughout most of this chapter, monetary policy is implicitly described in terms of money-supply targeting. Yet, the simulation results described in Section 5 refer to an increase in the Federal Funds rate. The transition can be made by indicating to students that the Fed may opt to conduct monetary policy by setting a target for the interest rate and adjusting the money supply to offset changes in money demand brought about by changes in Y. In effect, this policy would make the LM curve horizontal at the targeted interest rate. One could then investigate the consequences of changing the interest-rate target. This is effectively the analysis of Section 5.

VII. Observations

1. Conceptual Observations

i. The interest rate plays a critical role in the closed-economy IS-LM model. First, the interest rate is the channel through which monetary policy affects output. Second, the effect of fiscal policy on the interest rate limits the ability of fiscal policy to influence output. On the latter point, it is worthwhile to compare the output effects of an increase in *G* in the Keynesian cross model (modified to include endogenous investment) to the effects of the same policy in the IS-LM model. An increase in *G* shifts the IS curve to the right. The horizontal shift at the initial interest rate is the change in output from the Keynesian cross (see Figure 5.2). Clearly this is larger than the change in output from the IS-LM model, unless the LM curve is horizontal. In the IS-LM model, the increase in G leads to an increase in the interest rate, which tends to reduce investment. The interest rate effect is not present in the simple Keynesian cross model.

Figure 5.2: Fiscal Policy in the Keynesian Cross and the IS-LM Models

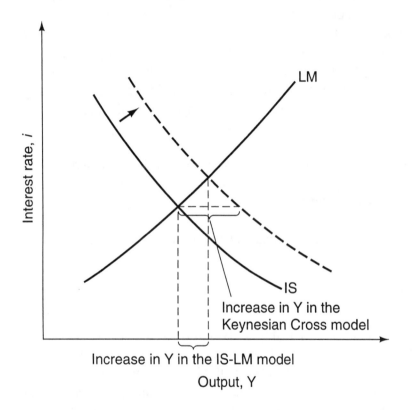

ii. The discussion of fiscal policy in the IS-LM model makes no reference to the implications of bond-financed government expenditures. Essentially, the text assumes that the flow effects (on the stock of bonds) from deficit financing are small enough to be ignored. The larger issue of Ricardian equivalence—whether there is any difference for the macroeconomy between tax and bond financing of government expenditures—is taken up in Chapter 27, on fiscal policy.

Chapter 6. The Labor Market

I.   Motivating Question

How Is the Unemployment Rate Determined in the Medium Run?

In the medium run, the unemployment rate tends to return to the so-called natural rate, determined by equilibrium in the labor market when the expected price level equals the actual price level. Conditional on correct price level expectations, equilibrium in the labor market occurs when the real wage implied by wage-setting behavior (influenced by the relative bargaining power of workers and firms) equals the real wage implied by price-setting behavior (influenced by the degree of competition in the goods market).

II.   Why the Answer Matters

The analytical framework in the text is built around equilibrium in three markets: goods, financial, and labor. Following the approach of Chapters 3 and 4, this chapter begins the discussion of the labor market by considering it in isolation.   The assumption that isolates the labor market from the other markets is that the expected price level equals the actual price level. In these circumstances, the framework presented in the book produces an equilibrium rate of unemployment and an equilibrium real wage, independent of the goods and financial markets. Unlike the other markets, however, the labor market considered in isolation is relevant not to the short run but to the medium run, a time frame over which it is reasonable to assume that price expectations are correct. The task of Chapter 7, which discusses aggregate demand and aggregate supply, is to unite all three markets in general equilibrium, in both the short and medium run, and to consider the transition from the short run to the medium run.

III. Key Tools, Concepts, and Assumptions

1. Tools and Concepts

i. The chapter reviews the definition of key labor market terms introduced in Chapter 2 and introduces several new ones, including the **nonemployment rate, discouraged workers, separations, layoffs,** and **quits**.

ii. The chapter makes use of a **production function**.

iii. The chapter introduces **wage-setting** and **price-setting** relations.

iv. The chapter defines analytically the **natural rate of unemployment** and the **natural level of output**.

v. The chapter introduces the concept of an **expected price level**, the first expectation seen in the book.

2. Assumptions

i. The chapter assumes that labor is the only factor of production. The text maintains this assumption until Chapter 10, which introduces growth.

ii. The chapter assumes a constant returns to scale production function. This implies that, given fixed technology, the real wage is constant.

IV. Summary of the Material

1. A Tour of the Labor Market

The chapter begins by describing the U.S. labor market. The most important point is the discussion of flows in the labor market between the three states of labor market activity: employed, unemployed, and out of the labor force. The chapter notes that flows from out of the labor force into employment suggest that some individuals classified as out of the labor force may be discouraged workers, *i.e.*, people who have given up looking for work, but who would take work if they could find it. If this is the case, the unemployment rate may underestimate the number of people available for work. Some economists prefer to use the nonemployment rate as a measure of the state of the labor market.

2. Movements in Unemployment

The chapter develops three facts about the U.S. unemployment rate. First, since World War II, there has been a slight upward trend in the unemployment rate. Second, when the unemployment rate is high, the proportion of unemployed workers finding jobs is low. Finally, when the unemployment rate is high, the proportion of employed workers losing their jobs is high.[1]

3. Wage Determination

Wage bargaining between employers and employees takes many different forms. In some occupations, wages are determined by collective bargaining between unions and firms. In the United States, less than 25% of workers are covered by collective bargaining agreements. Highly or uniquely skilled workers (*e.g.*, athletes, entertainers) engage in individual bargaining with their employers. For jobs that require little skill, employers may make take-it-or-leave-it wage offers.

---

[1] The evidence on workers losing their jobs is really about job separations, which include flows from employment to unemployment and from employment to out of the labor force. In principle, job separations include quits as well as layoffs. The text argues, however, that it is likely that most quits are associated with a flow from one job directly to another and, thus, that most quits are not counted as job separations.

The text summarizes this complex bargaining process by focusing on two factors. First, wage outcomes depend on labor market conditions, which can be proxied by the unemployment rate. When the unemployment rate is high, it is relatively easier for firms to replace workers and harder for workers to find new jobs, so worker bargaining power is relatively low. Second, given the unemployment rate, there are institutional and structural factors that affect the bargaining power of workers relative to employers. These factors include, among other things, the generosity of unemployment insurance and the size of flows through the unemployment pool. When the flows are large—say, because many jobs are being created and destroyed in periods of substantial structural change—it is less costly to be unemployed, since it is easier to get a new job.

These points suggest an aggregate wage bargaining relation of the following form:

$$W = P^e F(\overset{-}{u}, \overset{+}{z}) \qquad (6.1)$$

The nominal wage depends on the price level, because both workers and firms care about the real wage. The nominal wage depends on the expected price level, because wages are changed infrequently, so the price level that matters is the one that prevails over the duration of the contract, which is unknown at the time the wage is agreed.

4. Price Determination

Assume that labor is the only factor of production and that firms operate under constant returns to scale. Then, the production function takes the form:

$$Y = N \qquad (6.2)$$

Since the text assumes that technology is fixed in the medium run, equation (6.2) sets the marginal productivity of labor to one.

Now assume that the goods market is imperfectly competitive, so firms have some market power. This implies that firms will set price according to:

$$P = (1+\mu)W \qquad (6.3)$$

W is the marginal cost of output and μ is a markup reflecting the degree of market power possessed by firms. In a perfectly competitive environment, $\mu = 0$.

5. *The Natural Rate of Unemployment*

If expectations are correct (*i.e.*, $P=P^e$), equations (6.1) and (6.3) yield two different expressions for the real wage:

$$W/P=F(u,z) \qquad\qquad (6.1')$$

$$W/P=1/(1+\mu) \qquad\qquad (6.3')$$

The text refers to the first of these equations as the wage-setting relation (WS) and to the second as the price-setting relation (PS). Conditional on $P=P^e$, labor market equilibrium requires that the real wage implied by WS equal the real wage implied by PS, or:

$$F(u,z)=1/(1+\mu) \qquad\qquad (6.4)$$

The value of u that satisfies equation (6.4) is called the natural rate of unemployment. The graphical solution is given in Figure 6.1. Note that WS slopes down, since an increase in the unemployment rate tends to reduce the relative power of workers in wage bargaining. The PS curve is flat as a result of the assumption of constant returns to scale in the production function. If the production function exhibited decreasing returns to scale, the price-setting relation would be upward sloping.

The natural rate of unemployment is the rate of unemployment that makes WS and PS consistent when $P=P^e$. It is a medium-run concept, because economists typically believe that workers and firms will not hold expectations that are systematically wrong for long periods of time. In the short run, the text does not assume that $P=P^e$, so the actual unemployment rate need not equal the natural rate of unemployment.

Moreover, the adjective natural is misleading. The natural rate of unemployment depends on labor market institutions and market structure. For example, an increase in competition in the goods market (a decrease in μ) would shift the PS line up and reduce the natural rate of unemployment. An increase in the z index—say, because of an increase in unemployment benefits or an increase in turnover in the labor market—would shift the WS curve up and increase the natural rate of unemployment.

Note that employment N is given by $N=(1-u)L$, where L is the labor force. Assuming that L is fixed, the natural rate of unemployment (u_n) defines a natural level of employment $N_n=(1-u_n)L$, which implies a natural level of output $Y_n=N_n$. The natural level of output is the level of output that would prevail if price expectations were correct and the labor market were in equilibrium. Like the natural rate of unemployment, the natural level of output is a medium-run concept. In the short run, the actual price level can differ from the expected price level, the actual unemployment rate can differ from the natural rate, and the actual level of output can differ from the natural level of output.

Figure 6.1: The Natural Rate of Unemployment

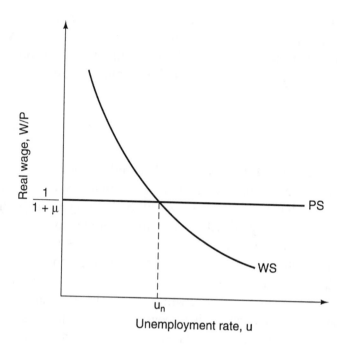

6. *Where We Go from Here*

This chapter discusses the determination of the unemployment rate and output in the medium run, when it is reasonable to assume that the price level equals the expected price level. In the short run, when the expected price level need not equal the actual price level, the demand factors discussed in the previous chapters affect the unemployment rate. The next three chapters incorporate the labor market into the model developed in the previous chapters and analyze the determination of output, the unemployment rate, and the interest rate in the short and medium run.

V. Pedagogy

1. *Points of Clarification*

The introduction of the expected price level, even in the simple fashion of the text, is a big jump for students. The text quickly removes the expected price level from discussion by equating it with the actual price level. As a result, students begin to think of the wage-setting and price-setting diagram as the method to determine unemployment at any time. It is worthwhile to emphasize that the natural rate is a medium-run concept and that there is no presumption that the price level equals the expected price level, or that the unemployment rate equals the natural rate, in the short run.

2. Alternative Sequencing

The second edition of the text moves directly from IS-LM to aggregate demand and aggregate supply. The first edition took up expectations after introducing IS-LM and then expanded the IS-LM framework to the open economy. The material in the second edition still allows instructors the option of considering expectations, the open economy in the short run, or both, before moving to aggregate demand and aggregate supply.

3. Enlivening the Lecture

From the instructor's point of view, an advantage of this chapter is that students will undoubtedly be acquainted with the labor market, probably more so than the other markets, at least at the relevant level of abstraction. Some students will have held jobs, a few will be looking ahead to their own employment possibilities after graduation, and virtually all will have family members or friends who have entered and exited the labor market for various reasons. Moreover, most will be familiar with the high profile wage bargaining of athletes and entertainers. So there is a rich base of personal experience and popular culture from which to draw to make the issues of this chapter more relevant for students. An extra emphasis on class participation may be more worthwhile in this chapter than any other. Possibly the most effective method to approach this chapter is to begin by asking students to describe their own job experiences, and use these experiences to illustrate as many points as possible about the labor market.

VI. Extensions

1. Supply and Demand in the Labor Market

A focus box in this chapter describes how the WS-PS analysis can be interpreted in terms of the supply and demand for labor. Instructors could also consider an alternative presentation, which does not assume $P=P^e$. Rewrite equation (6.1) in terms of the employment rate, N/L, and equation (6.3') in terms of the nominal wage:

$$W= P^e(1-N/L, z) \qquad (6.5)$$

$$W=P/(1+\mu) \qquad (6.6)$$

The first equation could be interpreted as a labor supply schedule in N-W space. It represents the wage that firms will have to pay to achieve a given level of employment, conditional on institutional factors z and the expected price level. One could think of equation (6.5) as describing the amount of labor workers would be willing to supply at various wages. However, this characterization is a bit misleading, because equation (6.5) does not concern the reservation wage, but the wage that results from a bargaining process. The second equation specifies the wage that firms are willing to pay, given the price level and the degree of competition in the product market. This equation can be interpreted as a labor demand schedule. It happens to be independent of the level of employment, because the text assumes a constant returns to scale production function. If the production function exhibited decreasing returns to scale, the labor demand schedule would have a negative slope.

Figure 6.2 plots equations (6.5) and (6.6), the latter for two price levels. Given z, the labor supply curve shifts when price expectations are revised. Given μ, the labor demand curve shifts when prices change. When $P=P^e$, the intersection of labor supply and labor demand determines the natural level of employment, N_n.

Figure 6.2: Labor Demand and Labor Supply

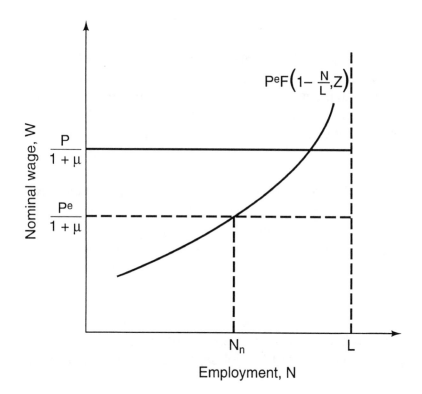

As Chapter 7 will discuss, the working assumption of the text is that changes in demand have initial, short-run effects on the price level, but not on the expected price level, which adjusts over time. Thus, changes in demand shift the labor demand curve and change the level of employment. For example, beginning from an equilibrium in which employment is at its natural level, an increase in demand increases the price level and shifts the labor demand curve up, so that $P/(1+\mu)>P^e/(1+\mu)$. This example is depicted in Figure 6.2. In the short run, as a result of the shift in labor demand, employment exceeds its natural level, and the unemployment rate falls below its natural rate. Over time, the expected price level adjusts, shifting the labor supply curve, and the price level adjusts further, continuing to shift the labor demand curve. In the medium run, when the expected price level equals the actual price level, labor supply and demand intersect at the natural rate of unemployment.

The complete characterization of labor demand and labor supply may be too advanced for students in the context of Chapter 6. However, it may useful to return to this characterization in Chapter 7, which discusses aggregate demand and aggregate supply. The characterization sketched above makes clear that employment (and, hence, the unemployment rate) is not always at its natural level, a point that students sometimes find difficult to grasp.

VII. Observations

1. Conceptual Observations

i. In the model developed in this chapter, the real wage is always determined by the price-setting relation, regardless of whether the actual price level equals the expected price level. Thus, the real wage is always determined by the degree of competition in product markets and the marginal product of labor, set equal to one in this chapter. Assuming that market structure and the level of technology change relatively slowly, the implication of this model is that real wages are fixed over the short and medium run.

ii. The natural rate of unemployment is the rate that satisfies two requirements: equilibrium in the labor market and correct expectations of the price level. It is a medium-run concept, because typically economists believe that price-level expectations are not consistently inaccurate over time. In the short run, however, price-level expectations may be inaccurate. Thus, in the short run, the actual rate of unemployment need not equal the natural rate of unemployment.

2. Empirical Observations

The most important empirical observations in this chapter concern the magnitude of flows in the U.S. labor market. For example, over the period from 1968 to 1986, job separations amounted to 3% of total employment each month.

Chapter 7. Putting All Markets Together: The AS-AD Model

I. Motivating Question

How Are Output, the Unemployment Rate, and the Interest Rate Determined in the Short and Medium Run?

Output, the unemployment rate, and the interest rate are determined by simultaneous equilibrium in the goods, financial, and labor markets. Simultaneous equilibrium in the goods and financial markets is summarized in an aggregate demand relation; equilibrium in the labor market is summarized in an aggregate supply relation. Labor market equilibrium is conditional on the expected price level. In the short run, the expected price level may not equal the actual price level, and thus the unemployment rate may not equal the natural rate. The text assumes backward-looking price expectations, so that, over time, the expected price level will tend to converge to the actual price level, and the unemployment rate will tend to return to the natural rate.

II. Why the Answer Matters

This chapter integrates the goods, financial, and labor markets in short-run and medium-run equilibrium. It is the culmination of the short-to-medium run model of the text, under the assumption that changes in monetary policy are discrete changes in the level of nominal money. The next two chapters introduce money growth and inflation into the analysis and begin to discuss the economy in terms of growth rates (except for the unemployment rate) rather than levels.

III. Key Tools, Concepts, and Assumptions

1. Tools and Concepts

i. The chapter introduces the **aggregate demand** and **aggregate supply** relations.

ii. The chapter makes extensive use of **dynamic analysis**.

2. Assumptions

The chapter assumes that the expected price level equals the price level of the previous period. This backward-looking expectations formation is essential for the dynamic analysis presented in the text.

IV. Summary of the Material

1. Aggregate Supply

Substitute the wage-setting relation into the price-setting relation to obtain:

$$P=P^e(1+\mu)F(u,z)$$

Express the unemployment rate in terms of output to derive a relationship between the price level and output:

$$P= P^e(1+\mu)F(1-Y/L,z) \tag{7.1}$$

Equation (7.1) is called the aggregate supply (AS) relation. For any price level, the AS relation gives the level of output consistent with equilibrium in the labor market, conditional on the expected price level, the degree of product market competition (μ), and institutional and structural conditions (z). As output increases, the unemployment rate decreases, the nominal wage increases (since workers are in a better bargaining position), and the price level increases (since price is a constant markup over the wage). Thus, the AS curve slopes up in Y-P space (Figure 7.1).

Along the AS curve, when output equals its natural level, the price level equals its expected level. This statement is true by construction. It is merely a restatement of the definition of the natural level of unemployment. When output exceeds its natural level, the price level exceeds its expected level. The high level of output leads to a low unemployment rate, which tends to increase the nominal wage and the price level.

The AS curve is shifted by the factors that influence labor market equilibrium. For example, an increase in the expected price level leads workers to bargain for a higher wage (for any given unemployment rate). The increase in the wage increases the price level through price setting. Thus, an increase in the expected price level causes the AS curve to shift up.

2. Aggregate Demand

Consider the IS-LM diagram from Chapter 5 (Figure 7.1). The diagram takes the price level, which affects the real money supply, as given. For given G, T, and M, an increase in the price level reduces the real money supply, shifts the LM curve up, and reduces output. Plotting all combinations of Y and P implied by the IS and LM model produces a downward-sloping relation, called the aggregate demand (AD) curve (Figure 7.1). For any given price level, the AD curve plots the level of output consistent with equilibrium in both the goods and financial markets.

The position of the aggregate demand curve depends upon the factors that determine the positions of the IS and LM curves. For a given price level, any change that increases output in the

IS-LM diagram will shift the AD curve horizontally to the right by the increase in output implied by the IS-LM model.

Figure 7.1: The IS-LM and AD-AS Models

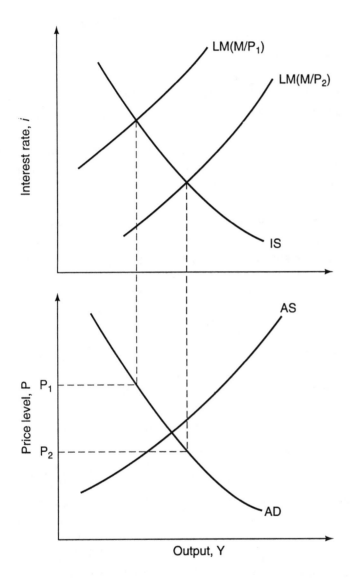

In symbols, the aggregate demand relation is given by:

$$\overset{+\quad-\quad+}{Y=Y(M/P,T,G)} \tag{7.2}$$

41

The signs above the arguments in equation (7.2) indicate the effects of an increase in the variables on output in the IS-LM model and, thus, the effects on the position of the AD curve.

3. Movements in Output and Prices

Figure 7.1 plots the AD and AS curves. The intersection of these curves is the short-run equilibrium of the economy. If it happens that $P=P^e$, then the economy is also in medium-run equilibrium. If $P \neq P^e$, then the text assumes that expectations will adjust. In particular, the text assumes that the expected price level is the price level in the preceding period, *i.e.*, $P^e_t = P_{t-1}$. Thus, if the price level at time t exceeds the expected price level, then the expected price level for time $t+1$ will increase to the price level at time t. The increase in the expected price level implies that the AS curve at time $t+1$ will shift up, relative to the AS curve at time t. This shift increases the equilibrium price level, which causes a further increase in the expected price level, another shift of the AS curve at time $t+2$, and so on. The geometry of this argument implies that the shifts of the AS curve will become smaller and smaller over time and that the expected price level will converge to the actual price level.

In general, when the price level is higher than the expected price level, the AS curve shifts up over time. When the price level is lower than the expected price level, the AS curve shifts down over time. The next three sections reinforce this point by considering the short- and medium-run effects of specific shocks.

4. The Effects of a Monetary Expansion

The effects of a monetary expansion are described in Figure 7.2. Suppose the economy begins in medium-run equilibrium, with the expected price level equal to the actual price level, and output at its natural level. An increase in the money supply shifts LM to the right in the top panel of the figure (to LM'), and simultaneously shifts AD to the right in the bottom panel. At the original price level, the horizontal shift of the AD curve (point B in the figure) equals the change in output in the IS-LM diagram before considering change in the price level.

The shift of the AD curve, however, tends to increase output, reduce the unemployment rate, and increase the nominal wage (through wage bargaining). The latter effect leads to an increase in the price level (through price setting). In other words, since the AS curve is upward-sloping, the new short-run equilibrium (point C) involves a higher price level. The increase in the price level tends to reduce the real money supply, and shifts the LM curve left (to LM"), offsetting some of the initial shift. Thus, in the short run, the output increase from a monetary expansion is less in the AD-AS model than in the IS-LM model. The increase in the price level offsets some of the effect of the monetary expansion on the real money supply.

42

Figure 7.2: A Monetary Expansion in the AD-AS Model

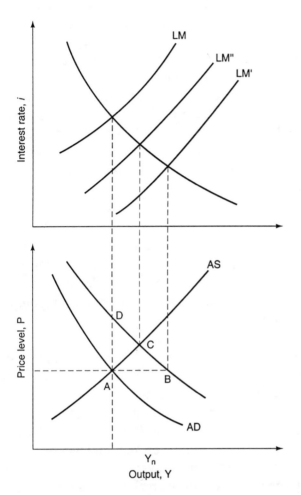

At the new short-run equilibrium (point C), the price level has increased above its expected level. As a result, in the next period, the AS curve will shift along the segment DC. Next period's AS curve (not shown in the figure) will pass through the point above Y_n corresponding to the price level that prevails at point C. This process continues with P rising each period until Y has been restored to its natural level at point D in the bottom panel and P has increased enough to restore M/P to its original value, which shifts LM back to its original position.

The new medium-run equilibrium is exactly the same as the original one, except that the price level has risen in proportion to the increase in M. The composition of GDP is the same as in the original medium-run equilibrium. Since, in the medium run, a monetary expansion affects only the price level and not any real variables, monetary policy (or in short, money) is said to be neutral in the medium run.

5. A Decrease in the Budget Deficit

A reduction in government spending shifts the IS and AD curves to the left. As a result, output and the price level fall. The decline in the price level generates a (relatively) small rightward shift of the LM curve, to make output in the IS-LM diagram consistent with output in the AD-AS diagram. As expectations adjust to the new price level, AS shifts down. The price level falls, but output begins to rise as the economy moves along the new AD curve. The AS curve continues to shift down until the economy reaches a new medium-run equilibrium, with a lower price level, but the same level of output as in the initial equilibrium. In the IS-LM diagram, the reduction in the price level shifts the LM curve to the right until it intersects the new IS curve at the initial level of output, but a lower interest rate. With output at its initial medium-run level, but the interest rate lower, investment will rise relative to the initial medium-run equilibrium. The rise in investment exactly offsets the fall in government spending.

6. Movements in the Price of Oil

The text models an increase in oil prices as in increase in μ, since higher energy costs increase the marginal cost of production, given the wage. The analysis of labor market equilibrium in Chapter 6 implies that the natural rate of unemployment will rise (the price-setting line will shift down), so the natural level of output will fall. Assuming that the economy begins in medium-run equilibrium, output will fall in the transition to the new medium-run equilibrium.

The AS relation in equation (7.1) implies that an increase in μ increases the price level for any level of output, so the AS curve shifts up. The new AS curve (Figure 7.3) will intersect the vertical line above the new natural level of output (Y_n') where the price level equals the expected price level (i.e., the original price level). As a result, in the new short-run equilibrium (point B in Figure 7.3), the price level has risen above the expected price level. Thus, the AS curve begins to shift up over time. The process continues until the AS curve intersects the original AD curve at the new natural level of output. In the new medium-run equilibrium (point C), output is lower and the price level is higher. In addition, in the IS-LM diagram (not shown), the increase in the price level reduces the real money supply and shifts the LM curve up, so the interest rate increases in the new medium-run equilibrium.

7. Conclusions

The exercises described in the chapter emphasize the distinction between the short-run and medium-run effects of shocks to the economy. Such shocks can arise from private behavior or from policy changes. Their dynamic effects are called propagation mechanisms. Fluctuations in output arise from the constant appearance of new shocks.

Figure 7.3: An Oil Price Increase in the AD-AS Model

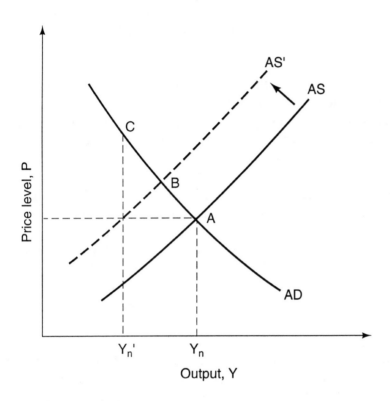

V. Pedagogy

1. Points of Clarification

i. Analysis of Shocks in the AD-AS Model

This is a difficult chapter. Students are likely to feel overwhelmed, particularly by the dynamics. To help students navigate the analysis of shocks in the AD-AS framework, instructors might find the following five-point guide useful.

i. Unless stated otherwise, assume that the economy begins in medium-run equilibrium. This implies that output is at its natural level, unemployment is at its natural rate, and the price level equals the expected price level.

ii. Determine whether the shock affects the natural rate of unemployment. If the shock is to a variable in the IS-LM model, it will not affect the natural rate of unemployment. If the shock is to a variable in the AS curve (other than the price level or the expected price level), it will affect the natural rate of unemployment and, thus, the natural level of output.

45

iii. Determine the initial shifts in the AD-AS diagram and IS-LM diagram. Do not neglect the secondary shift in the IS-LM diagram because of the change in price in the AD-AS diagram.

iv. Determine whether the price level is greater than its expected level or less than its expected level. If the economy begins in medium-run equilibrium, the expected price level is the initial price level.

v. If the price level is greater than its expected level, then the AS curve will shift up over time until it intersects the (possibly new) AD curve at the (possibly new) natural level of output. Likewise, as the price level increases over time, the LM curve will shift up until it intersects the (possibly new) IS curve at the (possibly new) natural level of output. If the price level is less than its expected level, the AS and LM curves will shift down.

It is also useful to clarify that the short-run, medium-run distinction is an analytical aid to help economists analyze the effects of shocks occurring at some point in time. In the real world, the economy is always experiencing some short-run shock and responding to previous shocks. The medium-run equilibrium describes a point to which the economy will tend to return in the absence of further shocks. The actual path of the economy, however, will depend on the sequence of shocks it receives.

ii. The Natural Rate Hypothesis

Instructors may wish to say more about the natural rate hypothesis, as described in the context of the AD-AS model, and explain the relationship between this hypothesis and the assumptions imposed in this chapter. The natural rate hypothesis typically has three elements. First, a natural rate exists, *i.e.*, when the price level equals its expected price level, there is a unique unemployment rate consistent with labor market equilibrium. In the context of the model developed in Chapter 6 (in which wage setting implies a negative relationship between nominal wages and the unemployment rate), the existence of a natural rate is guaranteed by the assumption that wages (in the wage setting relation) are proportional to expected prices. Second, the economy tends to return to the natural rate after shocks. In the AD-AS model, this result is generated by the assumption that the expected price level equals the lagged price level. Finally, the natural rate is reasonably stable, in the sense that it does not change so rapidly that economists can never measure it. Although the first two parts of the hypothesis could hold even if the natural rate changed very rapidly, the usefulness of the natural rate as a policy guide would be limited if it could not be measured with any confidence.

As will become more clear in Chapter 8, the main evidence in the United States for the first two parts of the natural rate hypothesis is that the unemployment rate has a significant negative relationship with the change in the inflation rate. The benchmark empirical specification (with the change in the inflation rate on the LHS of a regression) incorporates two assumptions—that wage inflation is proportional to expected price inflation (*i.e.*, that a natural rate exists) and that expected price inflation equals lagged price inflation. In reality, expectations formation is not all that well understood. At a minimum, expectations probably include some forward-looking elements. The text also notes that the natural rate can change over time and that relatively little is known about the determinants of the natural rate. If one accepts the stability of the U.S. natural rate since the 1970s, conventional techniques do not estimate it with much precision.

In sum, the natural rate hypothesis provides a powerful, unifying conceptual framework, but economists' understanding of labor market equilibrium remains limited.

VI. Extensions

Instructors may wish to relate the aggregate supply curve derived in this chapter to the aggregate supply behavior that had been assumed previously. Effectively, the IS-LM model assumed that the aggregate supply curve was flat. One could interpret a flat aggregate supply curve as a price-setting equation with a fixed nominal wage. The treatment in this chapter introduces a bit more realism into the description of the labor market by substituting the wage bargaining relation for the fixed wage. As a result of this substitution, the AS curve slopes up. When output increases, unemployment falls. Thus, given the expected price level, the wage increases (because the relative bargaining power of workers increases) and the price level increases (because price is a fixed markup over the wage).

VII. Observations

1. Conceptual Observations

In the medium run, the interest rate is determined by the intersection of the IS curve with the natural level of output. Effectively, conditional on the natural level of output, the interest rate is determined by fiscal policy. Regardless of the value of the money supply, the price level will adjust so that the LM curve intersects the IS curve at the natural level of output. Thus, monetary policy has no effect on the interest rate in the medium run. Once money growth is introduced, this statement will be refined somewhat. In the medium run, monetary policy will have no effect on the real interest rate, but it will affect the nominal interest rate through the Fisher effect (Chapter 14).

Chapter 8. The Phillips Curve

I.   Motivating Question

How Are the Inflation Rate and the Unemployment Rate Related in the Short and Medium Run?

Since about 1970, the United States data can be characterized as a negative relationship between the unemployment rate and the change in the inflation rate. This relationship implies the existence of an unemployment rate—called the natural rate of unemployment—for which the inflation rate is constant. When the unemployment rate is below the natural rate, the inflation rate increases; when the unemployment rate is above the natural rate, the inflation rate decreases.

II.   Why the Answer Matters

The material in this chapter provides a framework to think about the central issue of U.S. macroeconomic policy, namely, whether the Federal Reserve should change the interest rate (equivalently, the money supply) and if so, in what direction. As implied in the discussion in part I, according to the framework developed in this chapter, the economy cannot operate at an unemployment rate below the natural rate without a continual increase in the rate of inflation. This limits the ability of the central bank to stimulate the economy. By the same token, if the central bank wishes to reduce the inflation rate, it cannot do so without increasing the unemployment rate above the natural rate. The next chapter recasts aggregate demand in terms of the growth rate of money, develops a relationship between the unemployment rate and output growth, and considers in detail the policy tradeoffs facing the central bank.

III.   Key Tools, Concepts, and Assumptions

1. Tools and Concepts

i. The chapter introduces the original **Phillips curve** and its modern, **expectations-augmented** and **accelerationist** variants.

ii. The chapter expands the notion of the **natural rate of unemployment**. In the context of the accelerationist Phillips curve, the natural rate is the unique rate of unemployment consistent with a constant rate of inflation.   For this reason, the natural rate is sometimes called the **non-accelerating inflation rate of unemployment (NAIRU)**.

2. Assumptions

In the context of the modern Phillips curve, the chapter assumes that expected inflation equals lagged inflation. This assumption gives rise to the accelerationist Phillips curve.

IV. Summary of the Material

Prior to 1970, there was a negative relationship between the unemployment rate and the inflation rate in the United States. In the 1970s, this relationship broke down. Since 1970, the U.S. data can be characterized by a negative relationship between the unemployment rate and the change in the inflation rate. The original relationship is called the Phillips curve, after A.W. Phillips, who first discovered the relationship for the United Kingdom. The modern form is usually called the accelerationist or expectations-augmented Phillips curve.

1. Inflation, Expected Inflation, and Unemployment

Impose the specific functional form $F(u,z)=1-\alpha u+z$ and use the AS relation from Chapter 7 to derive:

$$\pi = \pi^e + (\mu + z) - \alpha u \tag{8.1}$$

Note that π^e refers to the expected inflation rate. An appendix to Chapter 8 presents the full derivation of equation (8.1).

The intuition for the relationships in equation (8.1) is the same as the intuition developed in the presentation of the aggregate supply relation. Given the price level in the previous period, an increase in the current price level implies an increase in the inflation rate, and an increase in the expected price level implies an increase in the expected inflation rate. Thus, an increase in the unemployment rate, which tends to reduce wages (because it reduces the relative bargaining power of workers) and thus to reduce prices (through the price-setting mechanism), also tends to reduce the inflation rate.

2. The Phillips Curve

Two explanations are commonly offered for the breakdown of the original Phillips curve in the 1970s. First, there were significant supply shocks in the 1970s. Since the Phillips curve is the aggregate supply curve in terms of inflation, supply shocks affect the Phillips curve. The oil price shocks in 1973 and 1979, which the text models as increases in μ, would have affected the original Phillips curve.

Second, the way workers form inflation expectations may have changed over time. The text models expected inflation as $\pi^e_t = \theta \pi_{t-1}$ and argues that it is plausible that θ was zero in the early postwar period (prior to the 1970s), when inflation was roughly zero on average. However, as the inflation rate increased, it is unlikely that workers failed to take notice. The text argues that the evidence supports a value of 1 for θ since 1970. Under this characterization of expectations, the original Phillips curve,

$$\pi_t = \mu + z - \alpha u_t \tag{8.2}$$

evolved to

$$\pi_t - \pi_{t-1} = \mu + z - \alpha u_t \tag{8.3}$$

Equations (8.2) and (8.3) describe fundamentally different relationships between the inflation rate and the unemployment rate. In the former equation, there is a permanent tradeoff between inflation and unemployment. In the latter equation, the unemployment rate is a constant when the inflation rate is constant or, more generally, when the inflation rate equals the expected rate of inflation. The unemployment rate defined by correct inflation expectations is called the natural rate of unemployment. To derive the natural rate, solve for the unemployment rate when the inflation rate is constant in equation (8.3) (or when the expected inflation rate equals the actual inflation rate in equation (8.1)):

$$u_n = (\mu + z)/\alpha \tag{8.4}$$

3. A Summary and Many Warnings

The text notes three limits on the use of the accelerationist Phillips curve in equation (8.1) as a characterization of the economy. First, the relationship between inflation and unemployment is likely to change at high levels of inflation. For example, when inflation is very high, wage indexation becomes more prevalent. The text models wage indexation as an automatic change in wages in proportion to current prices. Suppose that a share λ of wages in the economy are indexed to the actual inflation level, and the remainder are set according to expected inflation, assumed to equal past inflation. In this case, the Philllips curve becomes:

$$\pi_t = \lambda \pi_t + (1-\lambda) \pi_{t-1} + (\mu + z) - \alpha u$$

or

$$\pi_t - \pi_{t-1} = (\mu + z)/(1-\lambda) - [\alpha/(1-\lambda)] u \tag{8.5}$$

Indexation increases the effect of the unemployment rate on the inflation rate.

Second, within the context of the model developed in the text, the natural rate is not fixed. Institutional and structural factors in the labor market can affect the natural rate. In fact, available evidence indicates that the natural rate has differed across time and countries. It is difficult to identify the natural rate precisely at any point in time.

Finally, economists' understanding of the determinants of the natural rate is limited. The text notes, for example, that some economists believe that an oil price shock might affect the wage-bargaining relation in such a way as to offset its effect on the natural rate. Moreover, there is no consensus about the reasons for the apparent increase in the natural rate in Europe over the past twenty-five years or so.

V.   Pedagogy

The jump from the AS curve of Chapter 7 (in price levels) to the expectations-augmented Phillips curve of Chapter 8 (in inflation rates) may be difficult for some students. Chapter 7 itself required a big conceptual jump by analyzing wage-price dynamics. Chapter 8 may well seem to be something completely new. Time is required for this transition. It is useful to point out that the AS curve and the expectations-augmented Phillips curve essentially capture the same relationship, one in terms of the price level, the other in terms of inflation. A more subtle point is that the assumption that expected inflation equals lagged inflation is not equivalent to the assumption that the expected price level equals the lagged price level. The former assumption generates an equilibrium inflation rate (when embedded in the full medium-run model of Chapter 9); the latter generates an equilibrium price level.

VI.   Extensions

Instructors could introduce rational expectations by considering the consequences of $\pi = \pi^e$ in equation (8.3). Under this assumption, the unemployment rate equals its natural rate. Chapter 9 effectively discusses rational expectations, although it does not use the term, in the context of the credibility of monetary policymakers.

VII.   Observations

1. Conceptual Observations

In the medium run, there is no inflation in the AD-AS model. By contrast, the Phillips curve introduced in this chapter implies a constant (not necessarily zero) rate of inflation when unemployment is at its natural rate. The reason for this difference will become clear in the next chapter. In the AD-AS model, monetary policy is conceived in terms of the level of the money stock. In the medium-run model introduced in Chapter 9, monetary policy is conceived in terms of the growth rate of the money supply.

Chapter 9. Inflation, Activity, and Money Growth

I.   Motivating Questions

How Are Output Growth, the Inflation Rate, and the Unemployment Rate Determined in the Medium Run?

The medium-run economy consists of three relationships: the Phillips Curve, which links inflation and unemployment; Okun's law, which links output growth and unemployment; and aggregate demand (expressed in growth rates and simplified to include only the real money stock), which links money growth, inflation, and output growth. Medium-run equilibrium is characterized by a constant unemployment rate (the natural rate), a constant growth rate of output (the so-called normal growth rate), and an inflation rate which depends on the growth rate of money. In the medium run, the natural rate of unemployment and the normal growth rate of output are independent of money growth.

II.   Why the Answer Matters

Essentially, this chapter expresses the AD-AS analysis of Chapter 7 in terms of growth rates. This exercise matches the equations of the model with the observed relationships in the data and yields a fundamental result: in the medium run, money growth determines inflation, but does not affect output growth or unemployment. This framework allows for analysis of monetary policy decisions more closely related to real events than one-time changes in the money stock. The cost of disinflation and the scope for monetary policy to affect output are ongoing questions facing macroeconomic policymakers.

III.   Key Tools, Concepts, and Assumptions

1. Tools and Concepts

i. **Okun's law** is a negative relationship between the change in the unemployment rate and the difference between the growth rate of output and its normal rate, which is the sum of average annual productivity growth and labor force growth.

ii. A **point-year of excess unemployment** is one year of an unemployment rate one percentage point above the natural rate. The **sacrifice ratio** is the number of point years of excess unemployment required to reduce the inflation rate by one percent.

iii. The **Lucas critique** is the argument that historical relationships between macroeconomic variables may provide a misleading guide to the effects of policy changes, since the relationships may depend upon the policy environment.

IV. Summary of the Material

1. *Output, Unemployment, and Growth*

The dynamic model presented in this chapter has three ingredients: Okun's law, the Phillips Curve, and aggregate demand in growth rates.

i. Okun's Law

Okun's law is a relationship between changes in the unemployment rate and the growth rate of output. The model presented in the text, with no productivity growth and a fixed labor force, implies that the unemployment rate should fall when output growth is positive and rise when growth is negative (see the part VI for a formal derivation). In fact, the empirical relationship between the unemployment rate and output growth in the United States since 1960 is given by

$$u_t\text{-}u_{t\text{-}1}=\text{-}0.4(g_{y,t}\text{-}3\%) \tag{9.1}$$

where $g_{y,t}$ is the growth rate of output at time t. The observed relationship differs from the one implied by the basic model of the text in two fundamental ways. First, output growth must exceed 3% in order for the unemployment rate to fall. The growth rate required to maintain a constant unemployment rate is called the normal growth rate. Second, the coefficient on output growth is not -1, but -.4.

The 3% threshold for output growth arises from productivity growth and labor force growth. In the United States, productivity has grown by about 2% per year since 1960, and the labor force by about 1% per year. Productivity growth implies that fewer workers are required to produce a given quantity of goods. Thus, for employment to remain constant, output growth must match productivity growth. Labor force growth implies that unemployment will increase unless employment grows correspondingly. In sum, in order for the unemployment rate to remain constant, output must grow by 2% (to match productivity growth) plus 1% (to generate sufficient employment growth to match the growth rate of the labor force).

The coefficient of -.4 arises for two reasons. First, firms do not adjust employment one for one with output growth. Some workers are needed to operate a firm regardless of output. In addition, firms may hoard (not fire) workers in bad times to avoid the cost of training new workers in good times. Second, an increase in the employment rate tends to increase the labor force participation rate, which limits the effect of output growth on the observed unemployment rate.

ii. The Phillips Curve

The text uses the accelerationist Phillips curve from Chapter 8 for the medium-run model. For the United States, this relationship is roughly

$$\pi_t\text{-}\pi_{t\text{-}1}=\text{-}(u_t-6.5\%)$$

The coefficient on unemployment is -1, and the natural rate is about 6.5%.

iii. Aggregate Demand in Growth Rates

The final component of the medium-run model is aggregate demand. For simplicity, the text focuses on real money and writes aggregate demand as follows:

$$Y = \gamma M/P \tag{9.2}$$

Equation (9.2) implies

$$g_y = g_m - \pi \tag{9.3}$$

where g_m is the growth rate of money.

2. The Medium Run

Assume that the central bank maintains a constant growth rate of money, $\overline{g}_m$. In the medium run, the unemployment rate will be constant at the natural rate (the unemployment rate cannot increase or decrease forever), and output will grow at its normal rate. Equation (9.3) implies that the inflation rate will equal the growth rate of money minus normal output growth.

The implication of this analysis is that money growth affects only the inflation rate in the medium run. Money growth has no effect on medium-run output growth or unemployment. By the same token, inflation is ultimately determined by monetary policy.

3. Disinflation: A First Pass

The medium-run model can be used to analyze the mechanics of disinflation. Define a point-year of excess unemployment as one year of an unemployment rate one point above the natural rate. Define the sacrifice ratio as the number of point-years of excess unemployment required to reduce the inflation rate by one percentage point. The accelerationist Phillips curve implies a sacrifice ratio of $1/\alpha$, where α is the coefficient on the unemployment rate. In the United States, α is roughly equal to one, so the sacrifice ratio is roughly equal to one. Moreover, the linearity of the Phillips relation implies that the sacrifice ratio is independent of the path of the inflation rate. Thus, in the United States, a cumulative 10 percentage point reduction in the inflation rate implies 10 cumulative point-years of excess unemployment. The actual trajectory of the unemployment rate depends upon the trajectory of the inflation rate.

The purpose of the disinflation exercise is to determine the policy measures (the path of money growth) necessary to implement a desired path of inflation. The exercise assumes that the policymaker knows the natural rate of unemployment and the normal growth rate. The algorithm is as follows:

i. Identify the initial levels of the inflation rate, the unemployment rate, and output growth.

ii. Choose a desired time path of the inflation rate.

iii. For each year of the program, given the change in the inflation rate implied by (ii), use the Phillips curve to solve for the required unemployment rate.

iv. For each year of the program, given the change in the unemployment rate implied by (iii), use Okun's law to determine required output growth.

v. Use output growth and the inflation rate to determine the money growth rate required in each year to implement the policy.

4. Expectations, Credibility, and Nominal Contracts

In the mid-1970s, Robert Lucas argued that the disinflation analysis described above was likely to provide a misleading guide to the effects of policy. Necessarily, the estimated Phillips curve and Okun's law depend on historical data. Changes in policy, however, might change the historical relationships between variables. In particular, the way inflation expectations are formed might vary with the policy environment. This argument has come to be known as the Lucas critique.

The accelerationist Phillips curve assumes that expected inflation equals lagged inflation. In a disinflation, however, if the central bank could actually convince wage setters that it intended to reduce inflation, wage setters might expect inflation to be lower in the future than in the past. In the extreme, if the central bank announced its inflation target, and wage setters believed it, disinflation could be achieved without any increase in the unemployment rate above the natural rate. The accelerationist Phillips curve implies that unemployment equals its natural rate when expected inflation equals actual inflation.

The Lucas critique implies that credibility is an important determinant of the costs of disinflation. If policymakers can convince wage setters that a disinflation will be implemented, the policy can be carried out with relatively little increase in unemployment.

In response to the credibility argument, Stanley Fischer and John Taylor argued that the presence of nominal rigidities implied that even credible disinflations could be costly. Fischer emphasized that inflation would already be built into existing wage agreements and could not be reduced without cost. Taylor emphasized that wages were not all set at the same time. He argued that, assuming that workers cared about their wages relative to the wages of other workers, the existence of staggered wage contracts implied that wages (and, hence, prices) would adjust only slowly to changes in policy. As a result, a too rapid reduction in nominal money growth would lead to a less than proportional decrease in inflation. The real money stock would decline, leading to a recession and an increase in the unemployment rate.

In the late 1970s, using data on the pattern of wage contracts in the United States, Taylor estimated a path of disinflation for the U.S. economy that would not increase the unemployment rate.

The required disinflation began relatively slowly and increased over time. A problem with such a policy course, however, is that wage setters might not find it credible. Why should they believe a central bank that promises disinflation in the future?

5. *The U.S. Disinflation, 1979-1985*

The chapter concludes with an analysis of the Volcker disinflation, which began in the fourth quarter of 1979. The bottom line is that the sacrifice ratio was very close to what the disinflation analysis of the medium-run model would predict. There were no obvious credibility gains, even though Volcker had (and has?) a reputation as a tough anti-inflation fighter. Credibility theorists, however, can argue that Volcker lost his credibility when the Fed eased policy in 1980, in response to the recession.

V. Pedagogy

The task of calculating the policy path required to implement a disinflation may appear daunting to students. It is important to provide a recipe as well as intuition.

In addition, inflation is not a familiar phenomenon to U.S. students today. The Volcker disinflation episode is ancient history to them. Many will have never heard of Volcker. The cost of the Volcker disinflation can perhaps be cited as a factor that leads to fear of inflation—and the costs of disinflation—today.

VI. Extensions

Instructors could supplement the informal discussion of normal output growth with a formal derivation. Suppose $Y=AN$. Then,

$$\Delta Y/Y \approx \Delta A/A + \Delta N/N \tag{9.4}$$

The definition of the unemployment rate, $u=(L-N)/L$, implies that

$$\Delta u/u = (\Delta L - \Delta N)/(L-N) - (\Delta L/L) = [(1-u)/u][(\Delta L/L) - (\Delta N/N)]$$

or

$$\Delta u = (1-u)[(\Delta L/L) - (\Delta N/N)] \approx (\Delta L/L) - (\Delta N/N) \tag{9.5}$$

where the last approximation is valid if u is small. Substituting equation (9.4) into equation (9.5) implies

$$\Delta u = -(\Delta Y/Y - \Delta A/A - \Delta L/L)$$

Normal output growth is productivity growth ($\Delta A/A$) plus labor force growth ($\Delta L/L$). The unemployment rate declines when output grows faster than its normal rate.

VII. Observations

1. Conceptual Observations

An implication of the medium-run model of this chapter is that none of the variables that affected the price level in the AD-AS model has anything to do with medium-run inflation, unless these variables affect money growth. Budget deficits, for example, are sometimes financed by money creation. If so, they can affect inflation. Chapter 23, which looks at hyperinflation, describes how fiscal deficits can lead to money creation.

2. Empirical Observations

A. The text provides an estimate of one for the U.S. sacrifice ratio.

B. The Okun's law coefficient on output growth has traditionally been lower in European economies and Japan than in the United States, although the coefficients for Europe have been increasing over time. Indeed, the United Kingdom coefficient now exceeds the U.S. coefficient. These results are consistent with the notion that the U.S. labor market has traditionally been more flexible than the labor markets of other OECD economies, and that labor markets have been becoming more flexible worldwide.

Chapter 10. The Facts of Growth

I. Motivating Question

What Do Economists Know about Growth?

The chapter answers this question from two perspectives. First, it describes the empirical facts about growth across a spectrum of economies in the postwar period, with a brief discussion of growth over a broader time span. Second, it introduces an aggregate production function with constant returns to labor and capital together, but decreasing returns to each input separately. The chapter points out that this production function implies that growth cannot be sustained indefinitely by capital accumulation. Instead, technological progress is required.

II. Why the Answer Matters

Over the course of decades, the effects of output growth on economic welfare dominate the effects of output fluctuations. Understanding growth is of fundamental importance for the world's poorer economies, many of which have suffered negative per capita growth rates in the postwar period.

III. Key Tools, Concepts, and Assumptions

1. Tools and Concepts

i. The chapter introduces **logarithmic scales** for variable plots.

ii. The chapter develops an **aggregate production function** (modified to include capital) with **constant returns to scale** and **diminishing marginal products**.

IV. Summary of the Material

1. Growth in Rich Countries since 1950

Output per capita provides some measure of a country's standard of living. However, to compare per capita real output across countries, it is important to use a consistent set of prices for the goods produced in each country. Basic subsistence goods tend to be cheaper in poor countries than in rich ones, and subsistence goods account for a larger proportion of output in poor economies than in rich ones. Unless these price differences are taken into account, a comparison of real GDP per capita will tend to understate the relative real income of poor countries. GDP measures using a common set of prices are called purchasing power parity (PPP) numbers.

In terms of PPP numbers, there are three primary facts about growth in the G-5 economies (France, Germany, Japan, the United Kingdom, and the United States):

i. There has been a vast improvement in the standard of living in these economies over the past 45 years.

ii. The growth rate has decreased since the mid-1970s in all five countries.

iii. Levels of output per capita have tended to converge over time.

The last result could be an artifact of limiting attention to countries that have become rich. However, the convergence result seems to apply to the OECD countries in general and even to a broader set of economies. Not all economies have converged, however.

2. A Broader Look across Time and Space

From a broader historical perspective—say, the past 2000 years or so—growth rates achieved by rich economies between 1950 and 1973 seem exceptionally high. Moreover, the historical record seems more accurately described by leapfrogging than by convergence, since the identity of the richest country has changed several times since per capita growth became positive in the West (ca. 1400).

A closer look at the experience of a broad sample of 97 countries since 1960 reveals three facts:

i. OECD countries start at relatively high levels of output per capita and exhibit clear signs of convergence.

ii. Hong Kong, Singapore, South Korea, and Taiwan (the so-called Asian tigers) have also shown clear signs of convergence.

iii. There is no evidence of convergence for African countries, many of which have suffered negative growth rates in per capita terms since 1960.

3. Thinking about Growth

To think seriously about growth, it is necessary to modify the aggregate production function to include capital:

$$Y = F(\overset{+}{K}, \overset{+}{N}) \tag{10.1}$$

The function F defines the state of technology. It is assumed to exhibit constant returns to scale (CRS) and decreasing returns to labor and capital. The CRS assumption implies that equation (10.1) can be rewritten

$$Y/N = F(K/N,\ 1) \overset{+}{}$$ (10.2)

The decreasing returns assumption implies that the increase in output per worker from an extra unit of capital per worker will decline as K/N increases. Thus, the aggregate production function has the shape depicted in Figure 10.1.

Figure 10.1: The Aggregate Production Function

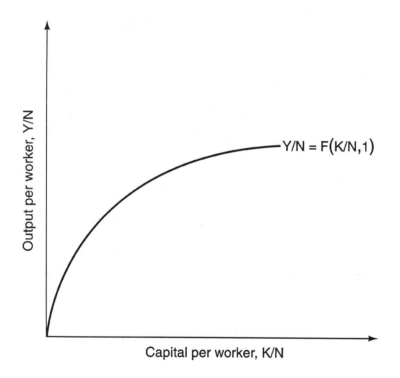

There are two potential sources of growth in output per worker. One is capital accumulation—increases in capital per worker—and the other is technological progress, which changes the F function so that a given value of K/N produces more and more Y/N. Capital accumulation cannot sustain growth indefinitely, however, because decreasing returns imply that larger and larger increases in capital per worker would be required. At some point, society would be unwilling to save the necessary resources to provide for the required increases in capital per worker, and growth would cease. Sustained growth requires sustained technological progress.

V. Pedagogy

The analysis of growth seems relatively disconnected from the material in the earlier chapters. One way to tie things together is to recall that Chapter 9, which assumed a production function without capital, defined the normal growth rate of output as the productivity growth rate plus the growth rate of the labor force. This definition implies that normal growth of output per worker equals productivity growth. Essentially, this chapter asks whether this definition must be modified when capital is included in the production function. In the long run, the answer is no. Over time, output growth is determined by productivity growth. Chapter 10 makes this point more formally.

VI. Extensions

Instructors may wish to address how the inclusion of capital would affect the analysis of the medium run developed in previous chapters. Essentially, the working assumption thus far has been that the capital stock changes very slowly, so it can be treated as fixed in the medium run. A fixed capital stock and a neoclassical production function (equation (10.1)) together imply that the firm's marginal cost curve rises with employment, since there are decreasing returns to labor. Thus, the markup over the wage will not be fixed, but will depend positively on the level of employment, as well as the degree of market power by firms.

VII. Observations

1. Conceptual Observations

The aggregate production function in the text is defined in terms of output per worker. If the ratio of employment to population is constant, then growth of output per worker equals growth of output per capita.

Chapter 11. Saving, Capital Accumulation, and Output

I. Motivating Question

Does the Saving Rate Affect Growth?

In the long run, saving does not affect growth, but does affect the level of per capita output. An increase in the saving rate can increase growth for some time, but not indefinitely, if the production function exhibits decreasing returns to capital per worker.

II. Why the Answer Matters

The comparatively low U.S. saving rate (relative to other OECD economies) becomes a policy issue from time to time and is discussed fairly frequently in the press. This chapter clarifies the relationship between saving, per capita output, and growth and discusses the likely effects of increasing the saving rate.

III. Key Tools, Concepts, and Assumptions

1. Tools and Concepts

i. The chapter develops the **Solow model** of growth for the case of no technological change and no population growth.

ii. The **golden rule** level of capital per worker is the value of capital per worker that maximizes steady-state consumption per worker.

2. Assumptions

This chapter assumes a closed economy, a fixed labor force, and a fixed level of technology.

IV. Summary of the Material

1. Interactions between Output and Capital

To save notation, write the aggregate production function of the previous chapter, $Y/N=F(K/N,1)$, as follows:

$$Y/N=f(K/N)$$

This step is valid because the second argument of the original function is a constant.

Now assume:

i. No technological change.

ii. Population, the labor force participation rate, and the natural rate of unemployment are all constant. Thus, N, interpreted as the natural level of employment, is also constant.

iii. The fraction of real GDP devoted to saving (the saving rate) is constant

$$S=sY \tag{11.1}$$

This assumption captures the empirical regularities that the saving rate (s) does not appear to change systematically as a country increases its income and that savings rates in rich countries do not appear to differ systematically from savings rates in poor countries.

iv. The economy is closed and the budget deficit is zero, so that goods market equilibrium is equivalent to

$$I=S \tag{11.2}$$

v) Capital depreciates at rate δ. Thus, the change in the capital stock over time is

$$K_{t+1}=(1-\delta)K_t+I_t \tag{11.3}$$

Investment creates new capital, but the existing capital stock depreciates.

2. Interactions between Output and Capital

The equations above together imply

$$(K_{t+1}/N- K_t/N)=sf(K_t/N)-\delta K_t/N \tag{11.4}$$

Capital per worker increases to the extent that total saving per worker exceeds depreciation of the existing capital stock per worker. Figure 11.1 plots the separate components of equation (11.4)

To the left of point A, investment per worker ($sf(K/N)$ exceeds depreciation of the existing stock ($\delta K/N$). Thus, the capital stock per worker (K/N) is rising. As K/N increases, output increases less than proportionately (given decreasing returns), and thus so does investment per worker. Depreciation, on the other hand, increases proportionately with capital per worker, so eventually an equilibrium will be reached at point A. At this equilibrium, capital per worker is constant, or, from equation (11.4):

$$sf(K/N) = \delta K/N \qquad (11.5)$$

Point A is called a steady state, since output per worker and capital per worker will stop changing. For this reason, time subscripts have been eliminated from equation (11.5). Point B determines steady-state output per worker, which is given by

$$Y*/N = f(K*/N) \qquad (11.6)$$

The dynamics of adjustment are indicated by the arrows on the horizontal axis of Figure 11.1. Note that if capital per worker were to begin above its steady-state value, K/N would fall, since depreciation of existing capital per worker would exceed total saving per worker.

Figure 11.1: Capital and Output Dynamics

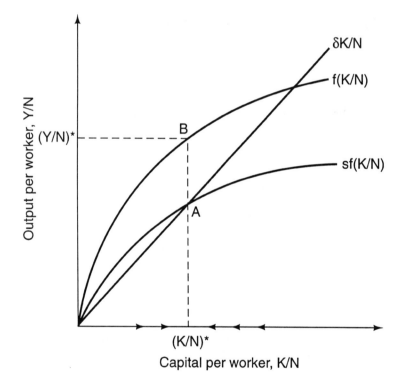

Now consider an increase in the saving rate. In Figure 11.2, an increase in the saving rate from s to s' shifts the $sf(K/N)$ curve upward in proportion to the change in the saving rate. The new steady-state equilibrium is given by point B. Notice that the steady-state growth rate (which is zero) is the same as the original steady-state growth rate. Capital per worker, however, is higher at point B, implying that output per worker is higher as well. These results imply that an increase in the saving rate will increase the growth rate temporarily, since output per worker must increase to reach the new steady state, but not in the long run.

What is the optimal saving rate? A very low saving rate will result in very low steady-state output and consumption per worker. A very high saving rate will waste resources on depreciation, since extra units of capital per worker produce very little extra output per worker when the capital stock is high. Somewhere in between is a saving rate that maximizes steady-state consumption per worker. This rate is called the golden rule saving rate, which produces the golden rule capital stock. Empirically, it appears that most countries have less than their golden rule levels of capital. This implies that increasing the saving rate could increase the consumption of future generations. On the other hand, an increase in the saving rate would reduce the level of consumption for some time, until the increased output generated by the higher capital stock compensated for the reduction in the proportion of output consumed.

Figure 11.2: Effects of Changes in the Saving Rate

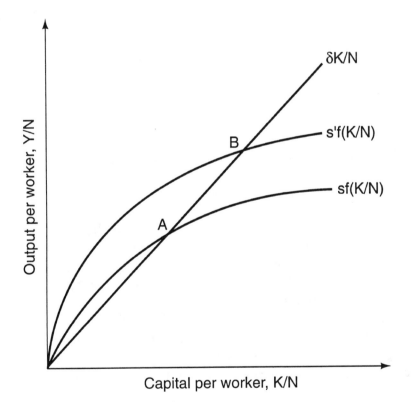

3. Getting a Sense of Magnitudes

A Cobb-Douglas production function with equal shares of labor and capital implies that the capital accumulation equation can be written

$$(K_{t+1}/N - K_t/N) = s(K_t/N)^{1/2} - \delta K_t/N$$

In steady state,

$$s/\delta = (K^*/N)^{1/2} = Y^*/N$$

In this case, a doubling of the saving rate leads to a doubling of output per worker in the long run. How fast does the capital stock increase? Suppose that s increases from 0.1 to 0.2, that the depreciation rate equals 0.1 initially, and that $K/N=1$. Using the dynamic equation (11.4), one can show that adjustment to the new steady state is only 63% complete after 20 years.

With the same Cobb-Douglas production function, consumption per worker can be written

$$C^*/N = Y^*/N - \delta K^*/N = (s/\delta) - \delta(s/\delta)^2 = s(1-s)/\delta$$

which is maximized when $s=1/2$. Almost all countries have saving rates below this level, which suggests that most countries have capital stocks below their golden rule levels.

4. Physical versus Human Capital

The aggregate production function can be generalized to include human capital (H):

$$Y/N = f(K/N, H/N)$$

The conclusions derived previously can be interpreted as applying to the accumulation of physical capital for given levels of human capital, or to the accumulation of human capital for given levels of physical capital. Whether increasing both factors in the same proportion would result in permanently higher growth is a subject of current research, associated with the "endogenous growth" literature triggered by the work of Lucas and Romer. The text argues that the evidence thus far does not provide much support for this proposition. One might draw from this conclusion that an increase in the human capital saving rate, *e.g.*, an increase in the proportion of output per worker spent on education, would not have permanent effects on the growth rate. On the other hand, it is possible that education might be related to the rate of technological progress. The next chapter looks at the sources and effects of technological progress.

V. Pedagogy

Students may be confused by the notion that an increase in the saving rate will increase steady-state consumption per worker, since IS-LM analysis suggests that an increase in the marginal propensity to save will reduce output. The differing results arise in different time frames, and both could be true. It may be worthwhile to clarify the short-run/long-run distinction in the context of this example. Moreover, the dynamic simulation in the text provides some idea of the length of the long run.

VI. Extensions

How could the introduction of human capital potentially allow for an increase in the saving rate to generate a permanently higher growth rate? The issue turns on whether the production function

$$Y/N = F(K/N,\ H/N)$$

exhibits constant returns to scale in its two arguments. If so, then equiproportional increases in human and physical capital per worker will generate proportional increases in output per worker forever. Thus, if the two types of capital are accumulated in equal proportion, an increase in the saving rate will generate a permanently higher growth rate.

VII. Observations

1. Conceptual Observations

Depreciation of the capital stock is necessary for the existence of a steady-state equilibrium in the growth model presented in this chapter. An increase in the depreciation rate would reduce the steady-state capital stock per worker.

Chapter 12. Technological Progress and Growth

I. Motivating Question

How Does Growth Relate to Technological Progress and What Determines the Rate of Technological Progress?

In the long run, the growth of per capita output equals the rate of productivity growth. Evidence from the postwar growth experience of five rich economies coincides with this assertion. Relatively little is known about the determinants of technological progress and specific policies that could increase growth.

II. Why the Answer Matters

Two fundamental economic issues hinge on an understanding of technological progress. First, why have many poor countries not grown in the postwar period and what can be done about it? Second, why has productivity growth slowed in the rich economies since the mid-1970s?

III. Key Tools, Concepts, and Assumptions

1. Tools and Concepts

i. **Effective labor** is the amount of labor multiplied by the level of labor productivity. In symbols, effective labor equals AN.

ii. **Growth accounting** is described in an appendix to the chapter.

2. Assumptions

This chapter continues to assume a closed economy, but allows for growth of the labor force and technological progress.

IV. Summary of the Material

1. Technological Progress and the Rate of Growth

Let the variable A denote the state of technology. Then write the aggregate production function as:

$$Y=F(K,NA) \tag{12.1}$$

This specification treats technological progress as a means to increase the amount of effective labor in the economy. As such, instead of describing the economy in terms of the ratios of capital and output to labor, it is convenient to describe it in terms of the ratios of capital and output to effective labor. With this substitution, the analysis proceeds as in Chapter 11.

The function F is assumed to exhibit constant returns to scale and decreasing returns in its arguments. It can be rewritten

$$Y/N=f(K/(NA)) \tag{12.2}$$

where the function f has positive but decreasing returns to $K/(NA)$.

With the government budget deficit set equal to zero, closed economy goods market equilibrium is equivalent to $I=S$, or in terms of effective labor,

$$I/(NA)=sf(K/(NA)) \tag{12.3}$$

In the model of Chapter 11, with a constant labor force and no technological progress, the capital-labor ratio reached a steady state when saving was just sufficient to replace capital depreciation. Since N was fixed, K/N was constant when K was constant, *i.e.*, when saving did no more than replace depreciated capital. In this model, in order for $K/(NA)$ to be constant, K must grow at the same rate as NA, so in steady state,

$$\Delta K/K=\Delta A/A+\Delta N/N\equiv g_A+g_N \tag{12.4}$$

which implies

$$\Delta K=(g_A+g_N)K \tag{12.5}$$

where g_A and g_N are the growth rates of productivity and the labor force. In order for equation (12.5) to hold, saving must be sufficient both to replace depreciated capital and to allow the capital stock to increase by $(g_A+g_N)K$. Thus, steady-state equilibrium (in units of effective labor) is given by

$$sf(K/(NA))=(\delta+g_A+g_N)K/(NA) \tag{12.6}$$

The economy looks qualitatively similar to Figure 11.1. In steady state, $Y/(NA)$ is constant, so output grows at rate g_A+g_N. Output per worker, however, grows at rate g_A. As before, an increase in the saving rate increases steady-state output per effective worker, but does not affect the steady-state growth rate.

2. The Determinants of Technological Progress

The model in this chapter establishes that long-run growth is determined by productivity growth, but takes technological progress as given. What are its sources? Technological change is the product of research and development (R&D), most of which is conducted by firms in search of increased profits. In general terms, R&D spending depends on the expected fertility of research (its yield of new ideas and products) and the appropriability of the benefits of research results. Fertility depends in part on the availability of basic research, but the relationship between basic research, applied research, and product development is not well understood. Appropriability depends on the degree of patent protection afforded to the inventors of new products. Policymakers must strike a difficult balance in formulating patent law. Too little patent protection may eliminate incentives to conduct R&D; too much may make it harder for future researchers to make full use of the gains of current research and may lead to too little R&D. In addition, the benefits to current consumers must be considered. Once a new product has been discovered, society would benefit from having the product available at cost. Patent protection allows the inventors of a product to enjoy a monopoly on its sale for a time, thus allowing the inventors to charge prices higher than cost, to motivate research effort.

3. The Facts of Growth Revisited

Chapter 10 described three basic facts: relatively high growth among the OECD countries from the 1950s to the 1970s, a reduction in the growth rate since the mid-1970s, and (except for the poorest economies) convergence. To explain these facts, the text compares measures of total factor productivity (TFP) growth with output growth for the G-5 countries. An appendix describes the Solow growth accounting methodology used to calculate the TFP measures. There are three findings, corresponding to the three facts. First, the high growth postwar period was marked by rapid productivity growth. Second, the reduction in growth since the mid-1970s is a result of lower productivity growth. Finally, convergence is a result of faster technological progress among poorer countries.

Why has productivity growth slowed? The text rules out three common explanations: measurement error, the transition to a service economy, and a decline in R&D spending. Measurement error in GDP has probably not increased over time, so it should not account for changes in productivity growth. The productivity slowdown has affected all sectors of the economy, so the change in the service share of output does not seem to explain it. Finally, R&D spending has not decreased. The remaining explanation is that R&D has become more fertile, but it is not clear why this has happened.

4. Epilogue: The Secrets of Growth

Although there has been progress in understanding growth, particularly in rich countries, economists still know little about how to affect the basic determinant of growth, technological progress. In particular, it is not clear what specific policies increase growth, why poor countries have failed to grow, and what lessons should be drawn from the experiences of the Asian economies that have achieved high growth rates. Moreover, as discussed above, the fall in productivity growth since the mid-1970s remains unexplained.

V. Pedagogy

The notion of a steady state in effective labor units may be confusing for students. The use of effective labor units as the numeraire is a mathematical convenience. The important measure of welfare is output per worker, not output per effective worker.

VI. Extensions

Instructors could remind students that, in a decentralized equilibrium, the real interest rate equals the marginal product of capital per effective labor unit minus the (fixed) depreciation rate. In steady state, the ratio of capital to effective labor units is fixed, so the real interest rate is fixed. Thus, the growth model determines the long-run real interest rate. This observation reinforces the notion that monetary policy does not affect the real interest rate in the long run, a result that provides some justification for the Fisher effect, discussed in Chapter 14.

VII. Observations

1. Conceptual Observations

The finding that the saving rate has no effect on the steady-state growth rate depends on the assumption that the size of the capital stock has no effect on productivity growth. This might not be true for human capital. Possibly, an increase in investment in education geared toward basic research could ultimately increase technological progress.

Chapter 13. Technological Progress, Unemployment, and Wages

I. Motivating Question

Does Technological Progress Create Unemployment?

In the medium run, the answer is no. If there is any relationship between productivity growth and unemployment, it is an inverse one. In the short run, the answer is theoretically and empirically ambiguous.

II. Why the Answer Matters

Chapters 10 through 12 established technological progress as the determinant of long-run per capita growth. Nevertheless, workers often fear that technological progress will eliminate their jobs. In response to this concern, Chapter 13 argues that productivity growth does not appear systematically to increase the unemployment rate. However, technological progress may create structural change, which could affect the distribution of income. Those workers with the wrong skills or tied to the wrong industries may lose.

III. Key Tools, Concepts, and Assumptions

1. Tools and Concepts

Essentially, there are no new tools in this chapter. The wage-setting, price-setting framework of Chapter 6 is adjusted to include productivity.

2. Assumptions

Since the focus of this chapter is unemployment, the text assumes that labor is the only factor of production.

IV. Summary of the Material

1. Productivity, Output, and Unemployment in the Short Run

To focus on employment issues, ignore capital, and write the production function as

$$Y=AN \tag{13.1}$$

An increase in A reduces the cost of producing a given level of output (because less labor is required), so the short-run AS curve shifts down. The effect on the AD curve depends upon the reason for the increase in A. The introduction of new technology may lead consumers to spend more, in expectation of higher future income, and may lead firms to invest more, in anticipation of higher future profits. These effects would cause AD to shift right. On the other hand, if the increase in A is a result of better use of existing technology, workers may worry about the safety of their jobs, leading them to save more. In this case, AD would shift left. Even if AD shifts right, the net effect on employment in the short run is ambiguous. It depends on whether output increases by a greater percentage than productivity.

Empirically, changes in output in the United States tend to be larger than changes in labor productivity. However, this fact does not imply that increases in productivity increase employment, because causation also runs the opposite way—from output growth to productivity growth—because of labor hoarding. Since firms tend to keep extra workers in bad times, measured productivity tends to increase in good times simply because firms make more use of their workers.

2. Productivity and the Natural Rate of Unemployment

In the medium run, unemployment returns to its natural rate, determined by the wage-setting and price-setting equations. Productivity growth affects both equations. Given the production function in equation (13.1), the marginal cost of production is W/A. Thus, the price setting relation becomes

$$P=(1+\mu)W/A \tag{13.2}$$

The text notes that empirical evidence suggests that wage setting reflects productivity growth. This observation suggests an extension of the wage-setting equation. Letting (A^e) denote expected productivity growth, the new wage-setting equation is

$$W=A^eP^eF(u,z) \tag{13.3}$$

When price and productivity expectations are correct, equations (13.2) and (13.3) become

$$W/P=A/(1+\mu) \tag{13.4}$$

$$W/P=AF(u,z) \tag{13.5}$$

73

The solution to these two equations implies that the natural rate of unemployment is independent of the level or growth rate of productivity (*i.e.*, A cancels out). In terms of the wage-setting, price-setting diagram of Chapter 6, an increase in A shifts the wage setting and price setting curves up by the same proportion at the initial natural rate of unemployment, so the natural rate does not change.

Empirically, a plot of decadal averages of labor productivity growth and the unemployment rate for the United States over the period 1890-1997 suggests that the two variables are basically unrelated. If anything, there may be a weak negative relationship (*i.e.*, when productivity growth increases, the unemployment rate falls). The negative relationship can be reconciled with the preceding analysis if expectations of productivity growth (which affect wage setting) lag behind actual changes (which affect price setting). If so, a period of slowing productivity growth would be associated with a higher natural rate of unemployment. To see this, suppose price expectations are correct, substitute A^e for A in equation (13.5), start from an original medium run equilibrium where $A^e = A$, and assume that A falls, so that $A^e > A$. Then, at the original natural rate (where $A^e = A$), the real wage demanded by wage setters exceeds the real wage paid by price setters. The natural rate will rise to reduce the real wage demanded by wage setters. When A^e falls to match the fall in A, the natural rate will return to its original value.

3. *Technological Progress and Distributional Effects*

The annual growth rate of the average real wage in the United States has been negative since 1979, despite the fact that productivity has grown by about one percent per year. To reconcile these numbers, the text notes that benefits have increased faster than wages and that the CPI, used to deflate wages for this calculation, has risen faster than the GDP deflator. The price-setting relation implies that productivity growth will be associated with an increase in wages divided by the GDP deflator.

The fall in real wages has not affected all workers equally. Real wages have fallen most for less educated and less experienced workers and more for men than for women. The increase in the relative wage of skilled versus unskilled workers reflects increased relative demand for skilled workers. Two common explanations for this phenomenon are increased international trade, which exposes low-skilled U.S. workers to foreign competition, and skill-biased technological progress. The trade explanation, however, does not explain why the relative demand for skilled workers seems to have increased even in those sectors not exposed to foreign competition. Given the growing differences between real wages across skill levels, firms may be motivated to explore new technologies that make use of low-skilled workers, and workers may be motivated to develop skills through investment in education. These developments would tend to mitigate wage inequality.

V.   Pedagogy

This chapter adds two modifications to the earlier discussion of the labor market. First, it extends the wage-setting equation to include the expected productivity level. Second, in the discussion of the short-run effects of technological progress, the chapter allows for the possibility that labor market shocks may affect aggregate demand. Instructors may wish to clarify the implications of these modifications.

Including the expected productivity level in the wage-setting equation in the manner of equation (13.3) implies that technological progress has no effect on the natural rate of unemployment, when this rate is defined by the conditions that price and productivity expectations are correct. Alternatively, if the wage-setting equation is not modified to include expected productivity, technological progress will certainly reduce the natural rate of unemployment in the wage-setting, price-setting model developed in the text. In this case, technological progress will shift the price-setting curve up, but have no effect on the wage-setting curve, so the natural rate or unemployment will fall. It is tempting to use this case as an interpretation of the apparent negative (although weak) relationship between productivity growth and unemployment. Interpreted strictly, however, this case would imply that productivity growth should steadily reduce unemployment.

In the short run, consider first the case where the expected productivity level equals the actual level. In this case, an increase in the productivity level implies an increase in the natural level of output, but no change in the natural rate of unemployment. The AS curve shifts down in the short run, and the equilibrium moves from E to E' in figure 13.1. If point E represents a medium-run equilibrium, than the shift of the AS curve implies that the price level has fallen below its expected level, so the expected price level falls, and AS shifts down further over time. Eventually, the AS curve intersects the AD curve at E'', where output is at its new natural level. Note that the transition from E' to E'' involves a reduction in the unemployment rate, since output increases but the productivity level does not change. Thus, since the unemployment rate at E'' is the same as the rate at E (*i.e.*, the natural rate has not changed), the unemployment rate must rise in the short run. In other words, absent changes in aggregate demand, an increase in the productivity level implies that the unemployment rate increases in the short run.

If technological progress is characterized by the development of new technologies, it may lead to increased investment and increased optimism about the future, effects which would shift the AD curve to the right. In this case, the short-run effect on unemployment is ambiguous; the effect depends on whether output increases by a greater proportion than productivity. On the other hand, if technological progress is characterized by better use of existing technology, workers may fear for the safety of their jobs and save more, an effect that would shift the AD curve to the left. In this case, the unemployment rate increases in the short run.

Apart from changes in aggregate demand, slowly changing expectations of the productivity level could also prevent a short-run rise in unemployment as a result of technological progress. The text discusses the implications of lagging productivity expectations in the context of the natural rate, but the analysis could also be applied to the short run. If the expected productivity level lags behind the actual level, it is possible for the unemployment rate to fall in the short run in response to an increase in the productivity level, even in the absence of a shift in the AD curve. However, if expected productivity ultimately catches up to actual productivity, so that the natural rate is ultimately unaffected by the productivity level, then a short-run decline in the unemployment rate must be followed by an increase back to the original natural rate.

VI. Extensions

These are described in the Pedagogy section.

VII. Observations

1. Conceptual Observations

According to the model of this chapter, the real wage is determined by the state of technology and the market power of firms. Increases in productivity increase the real wage; increases in the market power of firms reduce real wages.

Figure 13.1: An Increase in Productivity in the AD-AS Framework

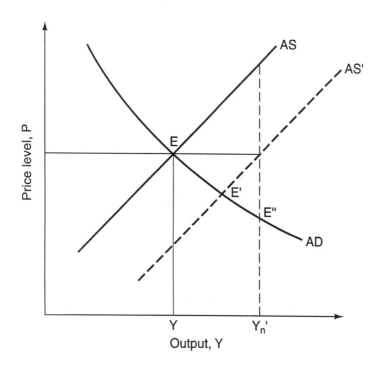

Chapter 14. Expectations: The Basic Tools

I. Motivating Question

How Can Consumers and Firms Compare Present and Future Economic Opportunities?

Future economic opportunities (payments received or made) can be expressed in terms of the present by using a discount factor, which acts like a price. The sum of a sequence of payments, each priced at the appropriate discount factor, is called the present discounted value of the sequence. In practice, future variables are not known, so one calculates the expected present discounted value, which is the present value of the expected sequence of payments.

II. Why the Answer Matters

Economic agents have foresight, so beliefs about the future can affect the present. This chapter describes the basic tools by which consumers and firms can price future economic events (payments made or received). In so doing, this chapter lays the groundwork for a look at consumption and investment decisions when agents are forward-looking, a discussion of asset markets, and an integration of expectations into IS-LM analysis. These topics are the subject of the next three chapters. Two important applications—the distinction between real and nominal interest rates and the effect of money growth on real and nominal interest rates—are analyzed in this chapter.

III. Key Tools, Concepts, and Assumptions

1. Tools and Concepts

i. The (expected) **real interest rate** measures the cost of borrowing in terms of goods, rather than money.

ii. The **expected present discounted value** of a sequence of payments is the value today (*i.e.*, in current nominal or real units) of the expected sequence of payments.

iii. According to the **Fisher effect**, in the medium run, money growth has no effect on the real interest rate, but a one-for-one effect on the nominal interest rate.

IV. Summary of the Material

1. Nominal versus Real Interest Rates

The nominal interest rate is the interest rate in terms of dollars. The real interest rate is the interest rate in terms of goods. The one-year real interest rate (r_t) is the cost, in terms of goods, of borrowing the equivalent of one good for a year. This cost is given by

$$r_t = P_t(1+i_t)/P^e_{t+1} - 1 \tag{14.1}$$

The first term on the RHS of equation (14.1) is the number of goods that have to be repaid at the end of the year. The second term is the number of goods borrowed at the beginning of the year. The repayment represents the expected cost (in terms of goods) of borrowing P_t to buy one good today. The nominal interest rate on the borrowed funds is i_t. Repayment is in terms of goods, so the nominal principal and interest payment has to be converted into goods at the future price. Since P_{t+1} is not known at time t, the expected repayment is expressed in terms of the expected future price level.

Defining the expected inflation rate (π^e_t) as $(P^e_{t+1}/P_t - 1)$, the real interest rate must satisfy

$$(1+r_t) = (1+i_t)/(1+\pi^e_t) \tag{14.2}$$

Equation (14.2) can be approximated as

$$r_t \approx i_t - \pi^e_t \tag{14.3}$$

2. Expected Present Discounted Values

An investment of \$1 today would grow to $(1+i_t)(1+i_{t+1})...(1+i_{t+n-1})$ in n years, if the investment proceeds were reinvested. Thus, to accumulate \$1 in n years, one would have to invest an amount

$$\$V_t = 1/[(1+i_t)(1+i_{t+1})...(1+i_{t+n-1})] \tag{14.4}$$

The required investment today is called the present value of \$1. This observation can be used to calculate the present value of any stream of future payments. Typically, however, neither future payments nor interest rates are known with certainty, so present value calculations must rely on the expected values of future payments and short-run interest rates. Sequences with constant interest rates and constant payments—over a fixed or infinite horizon—represent special cases. When future payments are expressed in real terms, they are appropriately discounted using current and expected future real interest rates.

3. Nominal and Real Interest Rates, and the IS-LM Model

The LM curve is unaffected by the distinction between nominal and real interest rates. Bonds earn real return $i-\pi^e$, and money earns real return $-\pi^e$. The difference in returns is the nominal interest rate, which is the rate in the LM curve derived previously. The IS curve, on the other hand, is affected by the distinction between real and nominal interest rates. Investment depends on the real interest rate. Suppose that firms must borrow to invest. Firms produce goods and care about how many goods they must repay, not how much money. Thus, the real interest rate should enter the investment function and the IS relation.

4. Money Growth, Inflation, Nominal and Real Interest Rates

Suppose the economy begins in a medium-run equilibrium with output at its natural level (Y_n), a zero growth rate of money, and zero expected and actual inflation. Since expected inflation is zero, the real interest rate equals the nominal rate. Now suppose the growth rate of money increases permanently to some level g_m greater than zero. How do real and nominal interest rates evolve over time?

Graphing the IS-LM model in Y-i space (Figure 14.1), an increase in money growth increases the real money stock in the short run, because prices adjust slowly. Thus, the LM curve shifts right (to LM'). As the price level increases, expected inflation is likely to increase, which tends to reduce the real interest rate, so the IS curve shifts right (to IS'). The vertical shift of the IS curve (in the short run) is the (short-run) increase in expected inflation. For a given level of output, each point on the IS curve gives the real interest rate consistent with goods market equilibrium. At any level of output, an increase in the nominal interest rate equal to the increase in expected inflation would leave the real interest rate unchanged and thus maintain equilibrium.

The combined shifts of the IS and LM curves imply that the real interest rate must fall in the short run. The effect on the nominal interest rate is theoretically ambiguous, but since the increase in expected inflation is likely to be small in the short run (implying a small shift of the IS curve in the short run), the nominal interest rate is likely to fall.

To think about the medium run, imagine replacing the nominal interest rate with the real interest rate on the vertical axis of the IS-LM diagram. In this case, the IS curve will be downward sloping. In the medium run, the real interest rate is determined by the intersection of the IS curve and the natural level of output. Since money growth affects neither the IS curve (graphed with the real interest rate on the vertical axis) nor the natural level of output, it cannot affect the real interest rate in the medium run. If output growth is zero, the model of Chapter 9 implies that money growth will equal the inflation rate in the medium run. Since expected inflation equals actual inflation in the medium run, the nominal interest rate will equal the real interest rate plus the growth rate of money. In other words, in the medium run, money growth affects the nominal interest rate one for one. This result is called the Fisher effect.

79

Figure 14.1: An Increase in the Growth Rate of Money in the Short Run

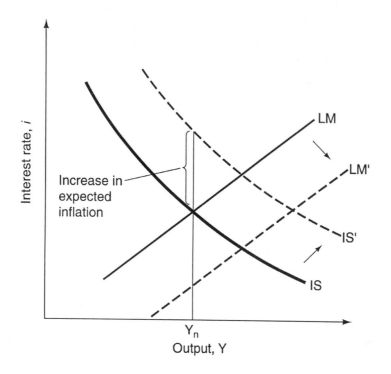

An increase in money growth also leads to fall in real money demand in the medium run, since the nominal interest rate rises but output does not change. Since real money demand falls, the real money supply must fall as well. In terms of the IS-LM diagram with the nominal interest rate on the vertical axis, in the medium run (Figure 14.2), the price level increases by a greater percentage than the nominal money supply, and the LM curve shifts up (to LM"). The IS curve shifts up as well (to IS"), since expected inflation increases. In the medium run, the vertical shift of the IS curve is equal to the growth rate of money, which is the actual and expected inflation rate. At the natural level of output, the vertical shifts of the IS and LM curves are the same.

How does the nominal interest rate fall in the short run yet rise in the medium run? The adjustment is driven by inflation dynamics and associated changes in inflation expectations. In the short run, the price level grows more slowly than the money supply. The real money supply increases, and the nominal interest rate falls. In addition, output increases above its natural level, which implies that the unemployment rate falls below its natural rate. The low unemployment rate triggers wage and price inflation, and eventually the price level begins growing faster than the nominal money supply, so the real money supply begins to fall. At this point, the nominal interest rate begins to increase. Over time, as the unemployment rate returns to its natural level, the inflation rate decreases, so the real money supply begins to fall more slowly. In the medium run, the inflation rate equals the growth rate of money, and the real money supply is constant. The level of the real money supply is lower than its initial level, however, because real money demand falls (the nominal interest rate increases and output does not change.)

Figure 14.2: An Increase in the Growth Rate of Money in the Medium Run

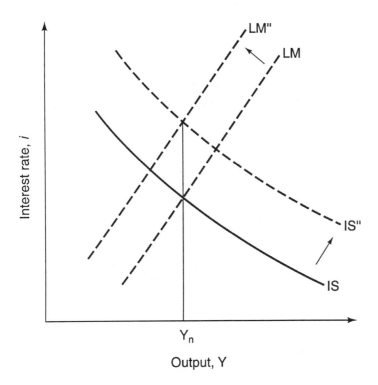

V. Pedagogy

This chapter marries two issues: the distinction between real and nominal interest rates and the calculation of expected present discounted values. Depending upon the focus of the course, instructors could make the distinction between real and nominal interest rates and ignore the mathematics of present values. It is also possible to discuss the effects of expected future policies (Chapter 17) without a full presentation of present value. In this context, instructors could describe informally how consumption and investment decisions (examined in Chapter 16) depend upon current and expected future income and interest rates.

VI. Extensions

The presentation of present value in the text assumes that economic agents are risk neutral. Although a formal treatment of uncertainty is outside the scope of the course, instructors might want to explain informally that attitudes toward risk affect the value of risky payment streams. In particular, distaste for risk tends to reduce the value of risky payments relative to the value of riskless ones.

VII. Observations

1. Conceptual Observations

The discount factor $d_t=1/(1+i_t)$ is a relative price that converts future dollars into present dollars. It plays the same role in present value calculations that market prices do in GDP. Likewise, the real discount factor, $1/(1+r_t)$, converts future goods into current goods.

2. Empirical Observations

The text constructs a series for the U.S. real interest rate by using a commercial forecast of inflation. Historically, economists have been unable to observe U.S. real interest rates directly. However, in 1997, the United States began offering Treasury bonds whose payments are indexed to the CPI inflation rate. The prices of these bonds allow economists to construct a direct measure of the U.S. real interest rate. A number of other countries also offer bonds with payments indexed to inflation. Chapter 15 provides a brief discussion of indexed bonds.

Chapter 15. Financial Markets and Expectations

I. Motivating Question

How Do Expectations Affect Asset Prices?

An asset is expected to provide a stream of future payments to the owner. Putting aside speculative bubbles, the value of an asset (its price) at any moment in time is the expected present discounted value of the stream of future payments. Putting aside risk, the expected real return on all assets should be the same; otherwise, investors would be willing to hold only the asset with the highest expected return. Since asset prices depend on expectations about the future, they are greatly affected by new information that changes these expectations. Likewise, the more unexpected an economic event— *e.g.*, a monetary policy decision—the greater its effect on asset prices.

II. Why the Answer Matters

At present, apart from the obvious topical interest in finance, the discussion of expectations and financial markets seems a bit of a sideshow. Chapter 16 will link asset prices and the real economy by introducing relationships between consumption and wealth and between investment and stock prices. Other chapters will discuss the possibility that a fall in asset prices can lead to a financial crisis, with repercussions for the real economy. In this context, Chapter 22 discusses the Great Depression and Chapter 24 the Asian Crisis.

III. Key Tools, Concepts, and Assumptions

1. Tools and Concepts

i. **Arbitrage** refers to the notion that (ignoring risk) expected returns on two assets must be the same. If two assets have different expected returns, investors will purchase the asset with the higher return and sell the one with the lower return, thereby increasing the relative price (and reducing the relative expected return) of the asset with the higher return. The process continues until expected returns on the two assets are equalized.

ii. A bond's **maturity** is the length of time over which it promises to make payments to the holder. A bond's **yield to maturity** is the constant interest rate that makes the present discounted value of future payments on the bond equal to the price of the bond today. The **yield curve** (also called the **term structure of interest rates**) is the relation between the yield to maturity and the maturity of a bond.

iii. The chapter introduces a significant amount of basic financial vocabulary.

iv. The **fundamental value** of a stock is the expected present discounted value of future dividends. A **rational speculative bubble** occurs when the stock price exceeds the fundamental value because investors expect the price to increase.

IV. Summary of the Material

1. Bond Prices and the Yield Curve

Bonds are assets that (typically) promise a sequence of fixed nominal payments. Ignore default risk, so that the promised payments actually occur. The price of a bond is the present value of these payments. For example, the price of a bond that promises to pay $100 in one year is given by

$$\$P_{1t}=\$100/(1+i_{1t})$$
(15.1)

The numeric subscript on the price and the nominal interest rate indicates a one-year bond. Note that the price of the bond varies inversely with the interest rate.

Likewise, the price of a bond that promises to pay $100 in two years (*i.e.*, a two-year bond) is given by

$$\$P_{2t}=\$100/[(1+i_{1t})(1+i^e_{1t+1})]$$
(15.2)

Note that price of the two-year bond (the present value of $100 received in two years) depends on the expected one-year interest rate next year.

An alternative derivation of the two-year bond price relies on arbitrage, the principle that expected returns on all assets (in positive supply) must be the same. If investors do not care about risk, as is assumed throughout most of the chapter, then no one would be willing to hold an asset with an expected return below the expected return on other assets.

Suppose investors choose between holding one- and two-year bonds. The one-year (gross) return on a one-year bond is $1+i_{1t}$. To derive the expected one-year (gross) return on a two-year bond, note that at the end of one year, the two-year bond will become, effectively, a one-year bond, with expected sale price $\$P^e_{1t+1}$. Divide this sale price by the original price to arrive at the expected one-year (gross) return of $\$P^e_{1t+1}/\$P_{2t}$. Equating the expected returns from the two assets and rearranging gives

$$\$P_{2t}=\$P^e_{1t+1}/(1+i_{1t})$$
(15.3)

The expected sale price of a one-year bond next year is simply the present value of the bond proceeds next year, or

$$\$P^e_{1t+1}=\$100/(1+i^e_{1t+1})$$
(15.4)

Substituting equation (15.4) into equation (15.3) gives the two-year bond price, which is identical to the price derived in equation (15.2).

The expression for the price of a two-year bond involves two interest rates: the current one-year rate and the expected future one-year rate. Likewise, the expression for the price of a bond that matures in n years would involve n interest rates. A summary measure of the return on n-year bonds is the yield to maturity, defined as the constant interest rate that equates the bond price with the present value of the future payments on the bond. The yield on an n-year bond is approximately equal to the average of the current one-rate interest rate and the expected one-year rates over the next $n-1$ years.

For example, the two-year bond yield (denoted by i_{2t}) is defined by

$$\$100/(1+i_{2t}) = \$P_{2t} = \$100/[(1+i_{1t})(1+i^e_{1t+1})], \tag{15.5}$$

which implies

$$(1+i_{2t}) = (1+i_{1t})(1+i^e_{1t+1}) \tag{15.6}$$

or

$$i_{2t} \approx (i_{1t} + i^e_{1t+1})/2 \tag{15.7}$$

The yield curve plots yields against bond maturities. The yield curve will slope up (yields will be higher on longer maturities) when financial market participants expect short-term interest rates to increase in the future. The yield curve will slope down when market participants expect short-term interest rates to decline.

2. The Stock Market and Movements in Stock Prices

Firms raise needed funds through debt (issuing corporate bonds or taking bank loans) and equity (selling ownership shares—stock—in the firm). Corporate bonds promise interest and principal repayments and are priced according to the methods described in part 1. Stocks, by contrast, have no predetermined payments. Periodically, the firm pays some of its profits as dividends to stockholders, but the amounts of these payments are under the firm's discretion.

Ignoring speculative bubbles, described in part 3, the price of a stock (denoted $\$Q_t$) is the expected present discounted value of future dividends. Thus, the ex-dividend price—the price after the current year's dividend has been paid—is given by

$$\$Q_t = \$D^e_{t+1}/(1+i_t) + \$D^e_{t+2}/[(1+i_t)(1+i^e_{t+1})] + \dots \tag{15.8}$$

where $\$D^e_{t+1}$ is the expected dividend next year. Note that the stock price must take account of dividends over the entire life of the firm. Equation (15.8) can be recast as an expression for the real stock price by replacing nominal dividends with real dividends and by discounting by real—instead of nominal—interest rates.

As described in an appendix to the chapter, the expression for the stock price can be derived from arbitrage between stocks and one-year bonds. Intuitively, arbitrage implies expected returns from stocks and bonds will be equalized. Thus, dividends will be discounted by bond interest rates (and expected interest rates). Moreover, the one-year return on a stock depends upon the dividend and the sales price of the stock after one year. The future sales price, however, will itself depend upon future dividends, so (again ignoring bubbles) the stock price can be written as an infinite series of discounted dividends.

Since stock prices depend upon expectations about the future, they change only when new information ("news") changes these expectations. As a result, apart from those cases where a few investors have better information than the rest of the market, changes in stock prices cannot be predicted. News that leads to increased expectations of output tends to increase stock prices, because higher output means higher profits and higher dividends. News that leads to increased expectations of interest rates tends to reduce stock prices, because higher interest rates make investment in bonds more attractive relative to stocks. In practice, a large part of the effect of news on the stock market is the market's evaluation of how the Federal Reserve will change policy in response.

For example, consider the response of the stock market to an unexpected increase in consumer spending. If the Fed is expected to do nothing, the response is ambiguous, because output increases (which tends to increase stock prices), but interest rates also increase (which tends to reduce stock prices). However, if the Fed is expected to increase the money supply to prevent interest rates from rising, stock prices will increase; if it is expected to reduce the money supply to prevent output from increasing (and thus reduce inflationary pressure), stock prices will fall.

In general, a monetary expansion will have very little effect on stock prices if it is anticipated, since expected dividends and interest rates do not change. To the extent that it is unanticipated, a monetary expansion will lead to an increase in stock prices, since it implies higher output (and thus higher dividends) and lower interest rates.

3. Bubbles, Fads, and Stock Prices

The present value of dividends is called the fundamental value of a stock. At times, stock prices deviate from their fundamental values. Sometimes this occurs for no good reason. Some financial investors may not be rational and may pay a high price for stocks simply because they have done well in the past. In contrast to these fads, sometimes stock prices exceed their fundamental values because investors expect stock prices to rise in the future. These episodes are called rational speculative bubbles. Even though a crash is possible when stock prices exceed their fundamental values, it may make sense for investors to pay a high price for stocks if there is a chance that prices will increase in the future.

Bubbles and fads are important because overpriced stocks are vulnerable to crashes, which can affect real activity.

V. Pedagogy

1. Points of Clarification

Bubbles cannot exist on bonds. The possibility of an asset bubble depends upon the price exploding (growing forever at too high a rate). Since bonds have a fixed terminal payment, there is no possibility that bond prices will rise forever.

2. Alternative Sequencing

This chapter is optional, even within the module on expectations. It is not required for most of Chapters 16 and 17. Moreover, instructors pressed for time could limit attention to bond pricing and the yield curve and omit discussion of the stock market.

3. Enlivening the Lecture

This chapter provides a wealth of possibilities to stimulate discussion in lecture. A useful tool is the yield curve, which is readily available in the newspaper and provides a good point of departure for a discussion of financial markets in the context of current economic events. Students might also appreciate a primer on reading the financial pages of the newspaper.

VI. Extensions

The main text assumes that investors are risk neutral. An appendix explores the implications of allowing for risk. Essentially, riskier assets are charged a risk premium (denoted by θ), which requires them to pay a higher expected return. As such, the risk premium acts as an increase in the discount rate, so that increases in the risk premium reduce stock prices. The text notes that the average risk premium on stocks over bonds has been about 5% in the United States over the past century and that the risk premium varies over time, contributing to variations in stock prices.

VII. Observations

1. Empirical Observations

Long-term interest rates tend to move in the same direction, but by a smaller amount, than short-term interest rates. Presumably, this fact reflects market expectations that part of the movements in short-term interest rates will be temporary.

Chapter 16. Expectations, Consumption, and Investment

I. Motivating Question

How Do Expectations about the Future Influence Consumption and Investment?

Consumers are to some degree forward-looking, and resources can be transferred over time through borrowing and lending. Therefore, in principle, consumption depends on wealth, rather than on income. Wealth includes the present value of expected future income, financial wealth, and housing wealth. Although income fluctuates over time, consumers, in principle, can maintain relatively constant consumption by borrowing when income is low and saving when it is high. To the extent that consumers are unable or unwilling to borrow when income is low, however, consumption will also depend on current income.

A firm decides to invest in a project when the present value of expected profits from the project exceeds its cost. Therefore, investment depends on expected future profits. In practice, the ability and desire of firms to borrow to finance investment may be limited when current profits are low. High current profits eliminate the need to borrow to finance investment. Therefore, investment will depend in part on current profits and in part on the present value of expected profits from a new project.

II. Why the Answer Matters

The discussion of economic fluctuations in the core ignored the role of expectations. This chapter sets the stage for a reexamination of the IS-LM model when expectations are taken into account. Chapter 17 addresses this task.

III. Key Tools, Concepts, and Assumptions

1. Tools and Concepts

i. The chapter introduces in passing the terms **permanent income theory of consumption** and **life cycle theory of consumption** to describe the consumption theory discussed in this chapter.

ii. **Human wealth** is the present value of expected after-tax labor income.

iii. **Tobin's q** is the ratio of a firm's financial value—the value of existing stock plus the value of bonds outstanding—to the replacement cost of the firm's capital. Theory and evidence suggest that Tobin's q should be positively related to investment.

iv. The **user** or **rental cost of capital** is the sum of the real interest rate and the depreciation rate on a unit of capital.

IV. Summary of the Material

1. Consumption

In earlier chapters, consumption was described as a function solely of current disposable income. In fact, however, people plan over longer horizons and are willing to borrow to finance current consumption when current disposable income is temporarily low. As a benchmark, assume that people want a constant flow of consumption over their lifetimes. In this case, a perfectly rational person would develop a consumption plan in two steps. First, she would calculate total wealth—assets on hand (financial and housing wealth) plus the present value of future labor income (so-called human wealth). Then, she would calculate the proportion of this wealth that should be spent each year to maintain a constant consumption level over her lifetime. If it happened that this level of consumption fell short of current income, the difference would be borrowed.

In practice, most consumers following such a plan would end up borrowing large sums of money early in life, because income during college and early working years is likely to be very low relative to income later in life. In fact, however, most young adults do not borrow the relatively large sums suggested by simple calculations, for several reasons. First, they may not intend to maintain constant consumption over their lifetimes. Some expensive leisure activities will be deferred, and plans will be made for higher expenditures while raising a family. Second, the computations involved in planning for constant consumption may be too complicated. Life is simpler when decisions are based on rules of thumb. Third, human wealth is based on forecasts of future earnings, which may turn out to be less than expected. Consumers may wish to protect against this possibility by borrowing smaller amounts than would be implied by expected present value calculations. Finally, banks may be unwilling to extend much credit to young adults on the expectation of future earnings.

This discussion suggests that consumption is likely to depend on two factors: wealth—because consumers are to some degree forward-looking—and current disposable income—because consumers may be unwilling or unable to calculate and implement a spending plan expected to maintain constant consumption over their lifetimes. Empirically, it is difficult to distinguish the relative importance of wealth and current disposable income in consumption decisions. Evidence suggests that the typical consumer does not begin thinking about retirement savings until sometime in his or her 40s. However, there are substantial differences in behavior across individuals.

The fact that consumption depends upon wealth (which in turn depends upon expectations about the future) has two empirical implications. First, fluctuations in current income are likely to generate less than proportional fluctuations in consumption. Unless a fluctuation in current income is permanent, human wealth (the expected present value of future labor income) will change less than proportionally, which implies that consumption will probably change less than proportionally as well. Second, consumption can be affected by changing expectations about the future, even when current income does not change.

2. Investment

When deciding whether to purchase a new machine or build a new plant, firms compare the expected present value of profits from the machine or plant to the cost. If the present value of profits exceeds the cost, they invest; if not, they do not invest. The calculation of the expected present value of profits requires not only a forecast of profits, but also a consideration of the wear and tear on the machine or plant from use. Wear and tear is called depreciation.

James Tobin pointed out that firms could use information available in financial markets to simplify the investment decision. The financial value of a firm (its stock market value plus the value of bonds outstanding) measures the value financial investors place on capital (plant and equipment) already in place. Firms should invest when the financial value of a unit of their capital exceeds the cost of an additional unit of capital. If firms behave in this way, there should be a positive relationship between aggregate investment and the ratio of the total financial value of firms to the replacement cost of their capital. The latter ratio is called Tobin's "q." In fact, there is a strong relationship between aggregate investment and a one-year lag of the q variable. This relationship does not imply that firms use the stock market to guide their investment behavior, however, since theory suggests that stock prices and investment decisions should be influenced by similar factors.

A convenient special case of the investment decision is described by the following scenario: the real interest rate is constant, and a new machine begins producing a constant annual (real) profit stream in one year's time and begins to depreciate at a constant rate in two years' time. In this case, in real terms, the present value of expected profits, denoted by $V(\Pi^e)$, is given by

$$V(\Pi^e) = \Pi/(r+\delta) \tag{16.1}$$

where r is the real interest rate and δ is the depreciation rate. The quantity $r+\delta$ is called the user cost or the rental cost of capital, since it represents the cost of renting a machine. The owner of a rented machine would require the same real return available on alternative assets—*i.e.*, the real interest rate—plus compensation for depreciation.

In general, investment depends upon expected future profits, but there is also evidence that investment increases when current profits increase, even after controlling for expected future profits. Firms with low current profits must borrow to invest. They may be reluctant to do so, since they may be unable to repay their debt if the future turns out worse than expected. They may be unable to do so, since lenders may not share the firm's optimistic assessment of its investment project. If a firm has high profits, it can retain some of its earnings for investment, eliminating the need to take on debt or find enthusiastic lenders.

Thus, investment should depend on current and expected future profit. What determines profit? The level of profit per unit of capital is likely to be closely related to the level of sales per unit of capital. Ignoring the distinction between sales and output, sales per unit of capital can be proxied by output per unit of capital. In fact, there is a close relationship between changes in profit per unit of capital and changes in the output-capital ratio.

3. The Volatility of Consumption and Investment

Although the consumption and investment decisions have some similarities, the theory developed above suggests that investment should be much more volatile than consumption. After an increase in income perceived as permanent, consumers would respond with at most an equal increase in consumption. After an increase in sales perceived as permanent, however, firms may respond by investing in projects many times larger than the increase in sales. In the absence of adjustment costs, firms have no reason to maintain a smooth flow of investment. Once projects become profitable, firms invest immediately. Consumers, on the other hand, desire to maintain a relatively constant level of consumption. In response to a permanent increase in income, it makes no sense for them to borrow to try to consume the entire future increase today.

In fact, although investment and consumption tend to move in the same direction, the movements of investment are much higher in percentage terms. In absolute terms, however, movements of investment and consumption are about the same, since total consumption is much larger than total investment.

V. Pedagogy

1. Points of Clarification

Instructors may wish to point out that what matters for investment is marginal—as opposed to average—profit. When evaluating an investment possibility, firms care about the expected extra profit that can be derived from employing one more unit of capital (marginal profit), rather than the expected profit per unit of existing capital (average profit). Marginal and average profit can differ.

2. Alternative Sequencing

Ricardian equivalence is discussed in Chapter 27, which is devoted to fiscal policy. Instructors could easily introduce Ricardian equivalence in this chapter, as well.

VI. Extensions

1. The Evolution of Consumption Theory

The text presents modern consumption theory, but does not describe how the Keynesian consumption function (KCF) came to be replaced by permanent income-life cycle theory. The story helps illustrate the differences between the KCF and the consumption theory described in this chapter.

The Keynesian consumption function (KCF) implies that the ratio of consumption to income (or the average propensity to consume (APC)) falls as income increases. Cross-section and time-series evidence assembled after the publication of the *General Theory* bore out these claims. Based on the KCF and the existing evidence, economists predicted during World War II that the economy could not sustain growth after the war without high levels of government spending. Since the consumption-output ratio would fall with income, some other component of output—in particular, government spending—would have to increase to support growth. To the surprise of many economists, the economy did not stagnate after the war, despite the associated fall in government spending. In addition, after the war, Simon Kuznets collected longer-run data that showed no tendency for the APC to decline secularly.

The theories of Friedman and Modigliani explained the apparent puzzle between the prewar and postwar evidence. The basic insight becomes clear in a simple example. Suppose that each year half of the population receives an income of $25,000 and the other half an income of $75,000. Those who receive $25,000 know they will receive $75,000 in the following year, and those who receive $75,000 know they will receive $25,000 in the following year. Everyone desires to smooth consumption completely, so everyone consumes $50,000 year. In aggregate, the relationship between income and consumption is stable and unchanging. In cross-section, it will appear that the ratio of consumption to income falls when income increases. Although there is no uncertainty in this example, the basic point is clear. The cross-section evidence largely reflects transitory changes in income, which have little effect on consumption. The aggregate evidence largely reflects the relationship between permanent income and consumption. In the long run, aggregate income is driven primarily by permanent changes in income, which tend to have close to proportional effects on consumption. So, in the long run, there is no tendency for the APC to decline.

2. Consumption and Real Interest Rates

The text does not discuss the effect of the real interest rate on consumption. An increase in the current period real interest rate has three effects. First, since the price of future consumption in terms of present consumption is $1/(1+r)$, an increase in the real interest rate reduces the relative price of future consumption and tends to shift consumption from the present to the future. Thus, current consumption tends to fall. Intuitively, an increase in the real return on bonds tends to make saving more attractive. Note that the benchmark of constant consumption is only a benchmark. The desire to smooth consumption is not absolute. Second, an increase in the interest rate increases the return on existing saving, which tends to reduce consumption. Alternatively, a higher interest rate means that any given level of future wealth can be achieved with less saving today, so consumption tends to rise. Finally, an increase in the current interest rate tends to reduce human wealth (the present value of expected after-tax labor income). This effect is larger to the extent that an increase in the current rate also implies an increase in future interest rates. The fall in human wealth implies a fall in consumption.

In sum, the theoretical effects are contradictory. The substitution and wealth effects predict that consumption responds negatively to the real interest rate; the income effect that consumption responds positively. Empirical studies do not find a strong relationship between consumption and the real interest rate.

VII. Observations

1. Conceptual Observations

Consumption depends in part on wealth. The text emphasizes the effects of human wealth on consumption, but fluctuations in the stock market and in housing prices can also affect consumption. At the time of this writing, part of the concern about the booming U.S. stock market was the potential effect on consumption in the event of a crash.

2. Empirical Observations

To reemphasize an important empirical point from the text, investment is much more volatile than consumption in percentage terms. Over the period 1960-1997, annual rates of change of investment range from plus 15% to minus 15%, and annual rates of change of consumption range from plus 4% to minus 4%. In absolute terms, however, movements of investment and consumption are about equal, since consumption accounts for a much larger share of GDP (about 68% in 1997) than does investment (about 14%, including residential investment).

Chapter 17. Expectations, Output, and Policy

I. Motivating Question

How Do Expectations Influence the Determination of Output and the Effects of Monetary and Fiscal Policy?

Consumption and investment are influenced by expected future output, and investment is influenced by the expected future interest rate. Since future monetary and fiscal policies affect future output and the future interest rate, expectations about future policy will affect output in the present. Moreover, the effect of current policy on output will depend on how current policy measures affect expectations about future policy.

II. Why the Answer Matters

This chapter ties together the section on expectations by incorporating expectations into the IS-LM model. It introduces rational expectations in an intuitive and natural way and allows relatively sophisticated discussion of the effects of monetary and fiscal policy.

III. Key Tools, Concepts, and Assumptions

1. Tools and Concepts

The chapter introduces **rational expectations** in the context of the IS-LM model by allowing economic agents to forecast the effects of future policy and to use these forecasts when determining current consumption and investment.

IV. Summary of the Material

1. Expectations and Decisions: Taking Stock

Think about time in terms of two periods: the present and the future, which lumps all future years together. Then, in the current period, the IS relation derived earlier in the text can be written

$$Y=A(\overset{+}{Y},\overset{-}{T},\overset{-}{r})+G \tag{17.1}$$

where *A*—which stands for aggregate private spending—is defined as consumption plus investment.

Introducing expectations requires thinking about the effects of expected future income (Y^e), expected future taxes (T^e), and the expected future real interest rate (r^e). Note that expected future government spending has no effect on the current IS relation, other than through its effect on future output and the future interest rate. From Chapter 16, an increase in expected future income will increase consumption and investment (since expected profits are likely to increase). An increase in expected future taxes will reduce expected disposable income, which will reduce consumption. An increase in the expected future real interest rate will reduce investment. Given these relationships, the IS curve can be rewritten

$$Y=A(\overset{+}{Y},\overset{-}{T},\overset{-}{r},\overset{+}{Y^e},\overset{-}{T^e},\overset{-}{r^e})+G \tag{17.2}$$

Given the values of expected future variables, the new IS curve remains downward-sloping in Y-r space, but it is likely to be steeper than the IS curve developed earlier in the book, for two reasons. First, given expected future interest rates, changes in the current interest rate have a relatively small effect on present values (of expected labor income and expected profits) and, thus, a relatively small effect on current spending (on consumption and investment), given income. Second, the multiplier is likely to be small, since, given expectations of future income, current income has a relatively small effect on consumption and investment.

The LM curve is unaffected by the introduction of expectations, since money demand depends on the current level of transactions. Money holdings can be adjusted in the future if the level of transactions change.

2. Monetary Policy, Expectations, and Output

For simplicity, assume that expected inflation is zero, so that the nominal interest rate equals the real interest rate. Then, the LM curve can be written

$$M/P=YL(r) \tag{17.3}$$

Now consider an increase in the current period money supply. Such an increase shifts the LM curve to the right and increases output and reduces the interest rate. In the absence of changes in expectations, the increase in output will be relatively small since the IS curve is steep. If, however, an increase in the current money supply leads people to expect an increase in the future money supply, expected future output will increase, and the expected future interest rate will decrease. Both of these effects cause the current period IS curve to shift to the right, increasing output further. Thus, the effects of policy depend on changes in expectations.

The preceding discussion relies on the sophisticated formation of expectations by economic actors. First they assess the likely course of future policy, and then they work out the economic implications. Expectations formed in this manner are called rational expectations. A box in the text describes the historical developments that led to rational expectations becoming the benchmark assumption in economics.

3. Deficit Reduction, Expectations, and Output

In the basic IS-LM model introduced in the core, a reduction in the government budget deficit reduced current output. Once expectations are introduced, the effect of deficit reduction on current output becomes ambiguous, because deficit reduction leads to a fall in the real interest rate and an increase in investment in the medium run and, thus, to an increase in output in the long run. In terms of equation (17.2), Y^e increases and r^e falls, both of which tend to shift the current period IS curve to the right. The direct effect of the deficit reduction—as a result of an increase in T or a reduction in G—shifts the current period IS curve to the left. The net effect on output—whether the current period IS curve shifts right or left—could be positive or negative.

This analysis suggests that a deficit reduction program is less likely to reduce current output to the extent that it is backloaded, *i.e.*, takes place further in the future, because the direct negative effects on output (through reduced government spending or increased taxes) would be postponed. On the other hand, a backloaded deficit reduction program may not be very credible. People may not believe that the government will follow through on politically difficult spending reductions and tax increases promised in the future.

A box in the text discusses Ireland's two attempts at deficit reduction in the 1980s. The first, in the early part of the decade, was associated with low growth and an increase in the unemployment rate. The second, in the latter half of the decade, was associated with high growth and a reduction in the unemployment rate. Some economists have argued that the second deficit reduction, which focused on spending cuts and tax reform, provides an example of an expansionary deficit reduction. They argue that the first deficit reduction, which focused on tax increases and did not change the size of the government's role in the economy, did not change expectations about the future very much. The text argues that evidence on the saving rate is consistent with this story. During the first deficit reduction, the saving rate rose, which suggests increased pessimism about the future. During the second deficit reduction, the saving rate fell, which suggests increased optimism about the future. On the other hand, monetary policy and other economic factors also differed between the two episodes, so the difference in results cannot be entirely attributed to expectations.

4. On to the Open Economy

This chapter concludes the first extension—expectations—to the model developed in the first twelve chapters. Chapters 18 through 21 address the second extension—the open economy.

V. Pedagogy

The presentation of the effects of expected monetary policy can be aided by drawing two IS-LM diagrams, one for the present and one for the future. First, work out the effects of expected future monetary policy in the IS-LM diagram representing the future. The changes in future output and the future interest rate show how expected future output and the expected future interest rate change. Use these effects on expectations to determine the effects on current variables in the IS-LM diagram representing the present. This technique ignores changes in expected inflation, but it does give a flavor for the effects of Fed watching on the economy.

The use of present and future IS-LM diagrams is less useful for illustrating the effects of expected fiscal policy, because changes in fiscal policy affect capital accumulation and output in the long run.

VI. Extensions

The first edition of the text used the Clinton deficit reduction package as an illustration of the design of deficit reduction programs. One point that emerged from this discussion was how expectations about the response of the central bank to deficit reduction affected the ultimate effect of the policy on output. Instructors might want to include the potential response of the Federal Reserve in the discussion of deficit reduction programs.

VII. Observations

1. Conceptual Observations

Once expectations are taken into account, the effect (on current output and the current interest rate) of a current change in an exogenous variable depends in part on how this change affects expectations about the future. Likewise, current output and the current interest rate can be affected by expectations about future changes in exogenous variables, even when no current exogenous variable changes.

Chapter 18. Openness in Goods and Financial Markets

I. Motivating Question

How Does Openness Modify the Closed-Economy, IS-LM, AD-AS Model?

An open economy allows domestic residents to choose between home and foreign goods and between home and foreign assets. The first choice is governed by the relative price of foreign goods; the second by relative returns on foreign assets.

II. Why the Answer Matters

For most countries other than the United States, open-economy considerations have substantial effects on economic performance. Even in the United States, discussions of the trade deficit often play a role in economic policymaking. This chapter describes the basic determinants of the trade balance and asset market arbitrage in international bonds. Chapter 19 integrates the trade balance discussion into the closed-economy goods market model (the Keynesian cross). Chapter 20 integrates the asset market discussion into the closed-economy model of the money market, and develops an open economy IS-LM model. Chapter 21 discusses a medium-run model of the open economy and considers exchange rate crises.

III. Key Tools, Concepts, and Assumptions

1. Tools and Concepts

i. The **nominal exchange rate** is the home currency price of foreign currency. The **real exchange rate** is the relative price of foreign goods. An increase in either of these variables is a depreciation from the perspective of the home country.

ii. The **balance of payments** is a record of one country's transactions with the rest of the world over a given period of time. The balance of payments consists of a **current account**, which records transactions in goods and services, and a **capital account**, which records transactions in assets. The chapter introduces basic balance of payments accounting and the balance of payments identity, which states that the current account and the capital account sum to zero.

iii. The **uncovered interest parity** condition equates the expected domestic-currency returns on domestic and foreign bonds. Absent transactions costs and assuming that investors do not care about currency risk, investors will not be willing to hold both domestic and foreign bonds unless uncovered interest parity holds.

2. Assumptions

i. The text assumes that domestic residents do not use foreign currency to purchase goods. This assumption is maintained throughout the formal work on the open economy. A footnote points out that U.S. dollars are sometimes used for transactions in economies with high inflation (or with a history of high inflation), but this phenomenon—dollarization—is ignored in the formal work of the text.

ii. The uncovered interest parity condition assumes that investors care only about expected returns and not about risk. This assumption is maintained throughout the formal discussion of the open economy.

IV. Summary of the Material

1. Openness in Goods Markets

Openness in goods markets means that domestic residents are able to buy foreign goods and sell domestic goods abroad. Goods sold to foreigners are called exports. Goods bought from foreigners are called imports. The difference between exports and imports is the trade balance. A negative trade balance is called a trade deficit, and a positive one a trade surplus. In the closed-economy model developed earlier in the book, domestic residents made only one decision—how much to spend. In an open economy, domestic residents make two decisions—how much to spend and how much to spend on domestic (as opposed to foreign) goods. The latter decision depends on the real exchange rate, the relative price of foreign goods in terms of home goods.

The real exchange rate depends on the nominal exchange rate (E), the foreign price level (P^*), and the home price level (P). The nominal exchange rate is defined as the home currency price of foreign currency. So, for example, if the United States were the home country, and one dollar traded for 100 yen, the nominal exchange rate would be 0.01 dollars/yen. Given this definition, an increase in the exchange rate means that the home currency loses value (*i.e.*, one unit of the foreign currency is worth more units of the home currency). A currency is said to depreciate when it loses value and to appreciate when it gains value. Thus, a depreciation (appreciation) of the home currency means an increase (decrease) in E.

Suppose Japan, the foreign country, produces only one good, cars. If a car were to sell for P^* in Japan, its price in dollars would be EP^*. Note that E is in units of dollars/yen and P^* in units of yen, so EP^* is in units of dollars. Now assume that the United States, the home country, also produces only one good, airplanes. One could compare the dollar price P of airplanes produced in the United States to the dollar price of cars produced in Japan. This motivates the definition of the real exchange rate (ε):

$$\varepsilon = EP^*/P \tag{18.1}$$

In this one-good-per-country example, the real exchange rate would have no units, since both the numerator and denominator would be expressed in terms of the home currency. In this case, the real exchange rate would be the price of the foreign good (in the foreign country) relative to the price of the home good (in the home country). Since there are many goods, in practice the real exchange rate is defined over baskets of goods, and P and P^* refer to price indices. As such, the real exchange rate is also an index: its level is arbitrary (since one can choose any base year for the price indices), but its rate of change is well defined. In terms of price indices, the real exchange rate measures the price of a basket of goods in the foreign country relative to the price of a basket of goods in the home country. Which basket depends upon which price index is used. If P refers to the GDP deflator, as in the text, then the real exchange rate measures the price of goods produced in the foreign country in terms of goods produced in the home country.

An increase in the relative price of foreign goods is a real depreciation (an increase in ε). An increase in the relative price of home goods is a real appreciation (a decrease in ε). Since a country has many trading partners, the bilateral real exchange rate defined above is often replaced by a multilateral real exchange rate, which is a weighted average of the real exchange rate against each of the country's trading partners. The weights are the shares of total home country trade with each country.

2. Openness in Financial Markets

Openness in financial markets means that domestic residents are able to exchange assets (stocks, bonds, and money) with residents of other countries. There is link between trade in assets and trade in goods. Trade in assets allows countries to borrow from one another. Thus, countries that run trade deficits can finance them by borrowing from countries that run trade surpluses.[1]

The balance of payments summarizes the transactions of one country with the rest of the world. It has two components. The first, the current account, is the sum of the trade balance, net investment income received from abroad, and transfers. As such, the current account is a record of net income received from the rest of the world. The second component of the balance of payments, the capital account, measures the purchase and sale of foreign assets. The capital account is defined as the net decrease in foreign assets (*i.e.*, the increase in home assets held by foreigners minus the increase in foreign assets held by home country residents). Apart from a statistical discrepancy, the current account and the capital account sum to zero by construction.

The intuition behind balance of payments accounting is simple. Think of a country as a single person. A country with a negative current account balance (a deficit) spends more than its income. To finance the deficit, it can either sell some of its existing assets to foreigners or borrow from foreigners (sell bonds to foreigners). By definition, these transactions have a positive sign in the capital account. Likewise, a country with a positive current account balance (a surplus) spends less than its income. It can dispose of the extra income by purchasing foreign assets or making loans to foreigners (buying foreign bonds). By definition, these transactions have a negative sign in the capital account.

The capital account measures a country's aggregate financial transactions with the rest of the world. Individual investment decisions are governed by the relative returns on home and foreign assets.

---

[1] Strictly, countries that run current account deficits borrow from countries that run current account surpluses.

The text assumes that domestic residents do not use foreign currency to purchase goods. Thus, there is no transactions motive for domestic residents to hold foreign currency. In addition, the text continues to assume that stocks and bonds are perfect substitutes, so it limits attention to home and foreign bonds.

How does one choose between home and foreign bonds? Suppose a U.S. resident has a dollar to invest. Let i be the interest rate on U.S. bonds and i^* the interest rate on Japanese bonds. Consider the choice between U.S. and Japanese bonds.

Option 1: Buy U.S. bonds

The return on one dollar equals $1+i_t$ dollars.

Option 2: Buy Japanese bonds.

    i. Exchange one dollar for $1/E_t$ yen.
    ii. Invest $1/E_t$ yen in Japanese bonds, with a return of $(1+i^*_t)/E_t$ yen
    iii. Exchange $(1+i^*_t)/E_t$ yen for $(1+i^*_t)E_{t+1}/E_t$ dollars.

The return on one dollar equals $(1+i^*_t)E_{t+1}/E_t$ dollars.
The expected return on one dollar equals $(1+i^*_t)E^e_{t+1}/E_t$ dollars.

Note that to transfer the return from the second option into dollars, the investor must exchange the return at the future period's exchange rate E_{t+1}, which is unknown at time t. The investor's expectation of the future exchange rate is given by E^e_{t+1}. If investors care only about expected returns and not about risk, then they will choose the option with the higher expected return. If both U.S. and Japanese bonds are to be held by the private sector, it must be that the expected returns are the same under either option. In other words,

$$1+i=(1+i^*)E^e_{t+1}/E_t$$

which can be approximated by

$$i \approx i^*_t+(E^e_{t+1}-E_t)/E_t \tag{18.2}$$

Equation (18.2) is called the uncovered interest parity condition. It is uncovered because an investor in foreign bonds is not protected from exchange rate risk. If the actual value of the exchange rate turns out to be lower than expected (*i.e.*, the dollar is more valuable than expected), the investment in Japanese bonds produces a smaller return than the investment in U.S. bonds.

In words, equation (18.2) says that the home interest rate equals (approximately) the foreign interest rate plus expected depreciation of the home currency. To make home assets attractive, foreign investors must be compensated for the expected depreciation.

3. Conclusions and a Look Ahead

Openness allows domestic residents two choices: the choice between home and foreign goods and the choice between home and foreign assets. Chapter 19 integrates the choice between home and foreign goods into the goods market equilibrium condition. Chapter 20 integrates the choice between home and foreign assets into the financial market equilibrium condition. Chapter 20 also combines goods and financial market equilibrium to analyze the short-run equilibrium of an open economy. Chapter 21 considers the medium run of an open economy and discusses exchange rate crises.

V.   Pedagogy

The study of an open economy imposes two important barriers to entry: exchange rate conventions and the balance of payments. As conventionally defined, an increase in the exchange rate is a depreciation for the home country. Although simple examples can make this clear, it will take time for this convention to become second nature for students. It is worthwhile to reinforce the exchange rate conventions often. Plotting actual exchange rates and relating the ups and downs to depreciations and appreciations can be helpful for this purpose

The balance of payments is presented only in a rudimentary fashion in the text. The intuition that (apart from investment income and transfers) a trade deficit means that a country spends more than its income will be reinforced in Chapter 20, which presents the GDP identify for an open economy. It is worthwhile to emphasize this intuition more than the text does. As far as the mechanics of balance of payments accounting, it may help build intuition to imagine that all payments are made in terms of home-country cash. In this case, transactions in which the home country receives a cash payment get a positive sign in the balance of payments. Transactions in which the home country makes a cash payment get a negative sign. For example, the purchase by a U.S. resident of a Japanese car requires a cash payment to Japan. This gets a negative sign in the U.S. balance of payments. The purchase of a U.S. Treasury bond by a Japanese resident requires a cash payment to the United States. This transaction gets a positive sign in the balance of payments.

VI.   Extensions

1. The Balance of Payments

The text omits several details of balance of payments accounting. An important one is that changes in official reserves are part of the capital account. Official reserves are foreign financial assets held by the central bank. For historical reasons, reserves include gold. An increase in reserves gets a negative sign in the capital account. Instructors may wish to explain how reserves fit into the balance of payments and to note that reserves affect the money supply. Doing so now helps prepare for a discussion of the central bank balance sheet in the context of fixed exchange rates (Chapter 20).

2. Uncovered Interest Parity

Although uncovered interest parity is a foundation of open-economy models, it has not been an empirical success. There are essentially two categories of explanation for this phenomenon. The first is that investors care about risk and there is a time-varying risk premium for any given exchange rate. The second is that investors make systematic forecast errors. Possibly forecast errors result from so-called Peso problems, *i.e.*, large-cost, low probability events. If the events occur very rarely, then it will often turn out (ex post) that expectations based on these events are incorrect (although not irrational). Instructors may wish to point out how a risk premium on a currency increases the interest rate paid on bonds denominated in that currency. Unfortunately, little is known about how or why the risk premium changes over time.

3. The Foreign Exchange Market

The text does not discuss alternative exchange rate regimes until Chapter 20. Instructors may wish to distinguish fixed, floating, and managed floating exchange rate regimes and to provide a brief history of the postwar transition from fixed to floating rates. Such a discussion fits naturally within the presentation of evidence on U.S. bilateral exchange rates in the postwar period.

VII. Observations and Exercises

1. Empirical Observations

i. In the United States, the export share of GDP is about 12%; in Japan, about 10%. Smaller European countries have much higher export shares.

ii. At the time of this writing, the United States has a substantial and increasing trade deficit. In the second quarter of 1999, the trade deficit amounted to 2.7% of GDP (Source: *Survey of Current Business*, BEA). Japan has a substantial trade surplus, roughly similar in magnitude relative to GDP, but less than half as large in dollar terms.

Chapter 19. The Goods Market in an Open Economy

I. Motivating Question

How Is Output Determined in the Short Run of an Open Economy?

As in a closed economy, output is determined by equilibrium in the goods market—the condition that goods supply equals goods demand. In the open economy, however, goods demand includes net exports.

II. Why the Answer Matters

The full treatment of short-run equilibrium in an open economy requires several steps. This chapter integrates openness in the goods market into the Keynesian cross model. To consider the goods market in isolation from financial markets, the chapter assumes that the interest rate is fixed, and considers the real exchange rate a policy variable. Chapter 20 integrates openness in asset markets into money market equilibrium, then combines goods and financial market equilibrium into an open-economy IS-LM model.

III. Key Tools, Concepts, and Assumptions

1. Tools and Concepts

i. The chapter introduces an **open-economy Keynesian cross** by adding net exports to the demand for domestic goods.

ii. The **Marshall-Lerner** condition ensures that a real depreciation will improve the trade balance. The condition, derived in an appendix, requires that the proportional change in relative prices (the proportional real depreciation) lead to a greater than proportional increase in relative quantities (the sum of the proportional increase in exports and the proportional decrease in imports).

iii. The **J-curve** describes the dynamics of trade balance adjustment after a real depreciation. Initially, the trade balance falls, since the real depreciation tends to increase the relative value of imports. Over time, however, consumers and firms start buying more home goods and fewer foreign goods (since real depreciation makes home goods cheaper), and the trade balance improves.

2. Assumptions

The chapter considers the short-run goods market in isolation from financial markets, so it assumes that the interest rate is fixed and that the real exchange rate is a policy variable. In keeping with the analysis of Chapter 20, as well as the closed-economy IS-LM analysis, a more precise way to state these assumptions is that the home and foreign price levels are fixed, and the nominal exchange rate is a policy variable. Since the price levels are fixed, the nominal exchange rate determines the real exchange rate. In addition, production is assumed to respond one-for-one to changes in demand without changes in price (the AS curve is horizontal at the initial price), so demand determines output.

IV. Summary of the Material

1. The IS Relation in an Open Economy

When the economy is open to trade in goods, it becomes important to distinguish the domestic demand for goods, given by $C+I+G$, from the demand for domestic goods, denoted by Z and given by

$$Z=C+I+G-\varepsilon Q+X \tag{19.1}$$

The domestic demand for goods is specified as in Chapter 5, *i.e.*, $C(Y-T)+I(Y,r)+G$. Real exports (X) and real imports (Q, measured in units of the foreign good) are given by:

$$X=X(\overset{+}{Y^*},\overset{+}{\varepsilon}) \tag{19.2}$$

$$Q=Q(\overset{+}{Y},\overset{-}{\varepsilon}) \tag{19.3}$$

Exports increase when foreign income (Y^*) increases, since foreigners have more to spend, and when there is a real depreciation (an increase in ε), since home goods become less expensive relative to foreign goods. Imports increase when home income increases, since home residents have more to spend, and when there is a real appreciation, since foreign goods become less expensive relative to home goods. Substituting equations (19.2) and (19.3) into the demand for domestic goods produces a new IS relation:

$$Y=C(Y-T)+I(Y,r)+G-\varepsilon Q(Y,\varepsilon)+X(Y^*,\varepsilon) \tag{19.4}$$

Note that real imports are multiplied by the real exchange rate to convert them into units of the home good.

Figure 19.1 displays graphically the effect of introducing net exports into the Keynesian cross model. The domestic demand for goods is denoted DD. To derive the demand for domestic goods, first shift the DD curve down by the value of imports (εQ). The new curve, denoted AA, is flatter than DD, because the value of imports increases with income. Now add exports to the AA curve to arrive at the demand for domestic goods (ZZ). Note that exports are independent of income, so the vertical distance between ZZ and AA is constant and the two curves have the same slope. The gap between the curves DD and ZZ is by construction the trade balance (sometimes called net exports (NX)), depicted in the lower panel in Figure 19.1. Since the value of imports increases with income, the trade balance decreases with income. Note that Figure 19.1 assumes that the real exchange rate is fixed.

Figure 19.1: The Demand for Domestic Goods and the Trade Balance (NX)

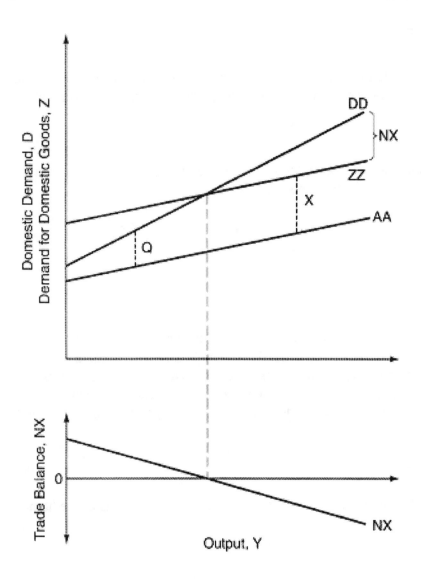

106

2. Equilibrium Output and the Trade Balance

Equilibrium in the goods market requires that the demand for domestic goods equals the production of domestic goods, namely that $Y=Z$. Since this chapter concentrates on the short run, it assumes that production responds one-for-one to changes in demand (without changes in price). Graphically, equilibrium is determined by the intersection of the ZZ curve and the 45°-line (Figure 19.2). In general, equilibrium does not require balanced trade. Figure 19.2 depicts an equilibrium with a trade deficit.

Figure 19.2: Equilibrium Output and the Trade Balance (NX)

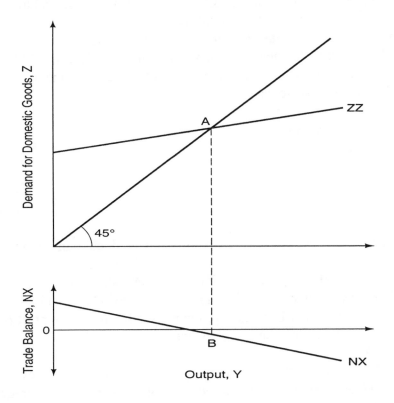

3. Increases in Demand, Domestic or Foreign

When domestic demand increases (*e.g.*, G increases, T decreases, or consumer confidence increases), output increases (point A moves to the northeast in Figure 19.2) and the trade surplus decreases (point B moves to the southeast). When foreign demand (Y^*) increases, the ZZ and NX curves shift up by the same amount. Output and the trade surplus increase. The increase in imports that arises from the increase in home output does not entirely offset the positive effect on exports from the increase in foreign demand.

Note that increases in domestic demand have a smaller effect on output in the open economy than in the closed economy, because some of the increased income "leaks" out of the domestic economy through spending on imports. In other words, the multiplier is smaller in an open economy. A box in the text carries this analysis further and notes that smaller countries are likely to have larger marginal propensities to import out of income. As a result, fiscal policy will have a smaller effect on output in a smaller economy, but a greater effect on the trade balance.

The relationship between foreign and home output suggests that policy coordination can be important when industrial countries as a group are operating below normal levels of output. Governments typically do not like to run trade deficits, because deficits require borrowing from the rest of the world. In the absence of coordinated action, an expansionary policy by an individual country in the midst of a worldwide recession will likely generate a trade deficit (or at least worsen the trade balance), because the increase in income will increase imports. Coordinated expansions will tend to have less effect on trade balances in individual countries, because imports will increase substantially throughout the world. On the other hand, coordinated expansions may be difficult to arrange. Countries that have budget deficits may be unwilling to consider expansionary fiscal policy. In addition, once an agreement has been negotiated, each country has an incentive to renege, thereby hoping to benefit from expansions abroad and to improve its trade balance.

4. Depreciation, the Trade Balance, and Output

The trade balance (NX) is given by:

$$NX = X(Y^*, \varepsilon) - \varepsilon Q(Y, \varepsilon) \tag{19.5}$$

A real depreciation has two effects: a quantity effect (an increase in exports and a reduction in imports), which tends to increase the trade balance, and a price effect (an increase in the relative price of imports), which tends to reduce the trade balance. The net effect will be positive if the Marshall-Lerner condition (derived in an appendix) is satisfied. If so, a real depreciation will improve the trade balance and increase output. With some qualifications, the Marshall-Lerner condition is usually satisfied in practice, and the text assumes that a real depreciation will improve the trade balance.

If the government can affect the real exchange rate through policy, then it can use two policy instruments (fiscal policy and the real exchange rate) to achieve two policy targets (output and the trade balance). For example, suppose a country in recession had a trade deficit, and policymakers wished to achieve a specific, higher level of output and balanced trade. Expansionary fiscal policy would increase output, but would also worsen the trade deficit. A real depreciation would increase output and improve the trade deficit, but there is no guarantee that it could achieve the output target under balanced trade. To achieve both targets, policymakers would need a policy mix. First, they would engineer a real depreciation sufficient to balance trade at the target output level. Then, they would use fiscal policy to ensure that the economy achieved the target output level. If output would be higher than desired after the real depreciation, than policymakers would use contractionary fiscal policy; if output would be lower than desired, they would use expansionary fiscal policy. The text includes a table that summarizes other policy mixes under alternative initial conditions for output and the trade balance.

5. *Looking at Dynamics: the J-Curve*

The effects of a real depreciation have a dynamic dimension. The price effect happens immediately, but the quantity effects take time. As a result, the trade balance tends to worsen immediately after a real depreciation, but improve over time. In other words, it takes some time for the Marshall-Lerner condition to be satisfied. This adjustment process of the trade balance—a temporary fall followed by a gradual improvement—is called the J-curve. Econometric evidence suggests that, in rich countries, the trade balance improves between six months and a year after a real depreciation.

6. *Saving, Investment, and Trade Deficits*

The national income identity (equation (19.1)) can be rearranged to read

$$NX=Y-C-I-G=(S-I)+(T-G) \tag{19.6}$$

where private saving (*S*) is given by $S=Y-C-T$. The first equality in equation (19.6) illustrates that the trade balance equals income minus spending. The second equality of equation (19.6) illustrates that the trade balance is the excess of private savings over investment plus the government budget surplus. Ignoring the distinction between the current account and the trade balance, a trade surplus implies that a country is lending to the rest of the world. The funds for this lending are derived from the two sources on the RHS of equation (19.6).

Since saving and investment are endogenous, equation (19.6) can be a misleading guide for policy analysis. For example, one might conclude from (19.6) that a real depreciation has no effect on the trade balance, because the real exchange rate does not appear. In fact, a real depreciation affects saving and investment, because it affects output. If the Marshall-Lerner condition is satisfied, a real depreciation will increase saving more than it increases investment, and improve the trade balance.

V.   Pedagogy

The open-economy saving-investment balance (equation (19.6)) is presented at the end of the chapter. There are two arguments for placing it at the beginning. First, the derivation of equation (19.6) illustrates that the trade balance is the difference between income and spending, an intuition that may not be sufficiently emphasized in Chapter 18. Second, by discussing equation (19.6) before the policy experiments, instructors can include the effects on saving and investment in the discussion of fiscal and exchange rate policy. This approach will reinforce the notion that saving and investment are endogenous and that the government surplus is not the only determinant of the trade balance. To illustrate the latter point, note that the U.S. federal budget deficit has declined over the 1990s, but the trade deficit has reached record levels.

VI. Extensions

The discussion of policy coordination in the text could be formalized. Suppose the world economy consists of two countries, home and foreign. The goods-market equilibrium conditions for the two countries can be written

$$Y=aY+F-qY+q*Y* \tag{19.7}$$

$$Y*=a*Y*+F*-q*Y*+qY \tag{19.8}$$

where a and $a*$ are the home and foreign marginal propensities to spend out of income, q and $q*$ are the marginal propensities to spend on imports, and F and $F*$ denote autonomous expenditure. Home imports, given by qY, equal foreign exports, and home exports equal foreign imports. Assume that initially $F=F*$, and the countries are perfectly symmetric, so that $Y=Y*$. The initial equilibrium is point A in Figure 19.3.

Suppose that point A represents desired or normal output levels for the two countries. Now assume that F and $F*$ fall by the same amount, reducing output by the same amount in each country, and moving the equilibrium to point B. Note that the trade balance remains at zero for both countries. If the countries coordinate policy, and increase F and $F*$ by the same amounts, the original equilibrium will be restored. On the other hand, if the home country increases F, but the foreign country does not, the new equilibrium will be at point C. Both Y and $Y*$ will increase, but since point C is above the 45°-line, Y will increase by more, implying that home imports will increase more than foreign imports, and home will run a trade deficit. In this case, the foreign country will have an increase in output without doing anything, and its trade balance will improve. Thus, there is some incentive for each country to let the other country undertake the burden of adjustment.

Figure 19.3: Coordinated Versus Uncoordinated Policies

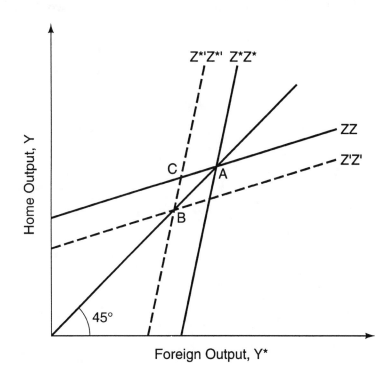

VII. Observations

1. Conceptual Observations

Real imports Q are measured in units of foreign goods. Suppose Japan is the foreign country and produces only one good, cars, and the United States is the home country and produces only one good, aircraft. The real exchange rate is in units of aircraft/car:

$$\varepsilon = EP^*/P = (\text{dollars/yen})(\text{yen/car})/(\text{dollars/aircraft}) = \text{aircraft/car}$$

Since Q is measured in units of cars, εQ is measured in units of aircraft, the home good. Thus, εQ is a proper measure of imports to include in the home real GDP equation, which measures all quantities in units of the home good. In a multi-good world, the same analysis applies, with "home production baskets" replacing "aircraft," and "foreign production baskets" replacing "cars."

2. Empirical Observations

In the United States, changes in the trade balance during the dollar depreciations of the 1980s (at the beginning of the decade and after 1985) tended to lag changes in the real exchange rate, as would be predicted by the J-curve.

Chapter 20. Output, the Interest Rate, and the Exchange Rate

I. Motivating Question

the Interest Rate, and the Exchange Rate Determined Simultaneously

e determined jointly by simultaneous
orld financial markets. In the open economy,
market allows trade between home and foreign
fferent implications for the relative
output.

by dropping the assumption that the exchange
, it adopts the short-run assumption that home
ge rate determines the real exchange rate. Since
ge rate affects output. To determine the
money market, which determines the home
which links home and foreign interest rates and

ions

dell-Fleming model, which is the IS-LM model
s treatment differs from the canonical model by
, rather than equal to the current rate.

xchange rate (akin to a depreciation). A
revaluation is a decrease in the level of a fixed exchange rate (akin to an appreciation).

iii. An appendix to the chapter discusses the **central bank balance sheet**, in the context of monetary policy under fixed exchange rates.

2. Assumptions

i. The home and foreign price levels are assumed to be fixed. Accordingly, expected inflation is assumed to be zero, so the real interest rate equals the nominal rate.

ii. Production is assumed to be perfectly price-elastic, so demand determines output.

iii. Foreign currency is assumed to have no transactions value for domestic residents.

iv. Home and foreign bonds are considered perfect substitutes and there is perfect capital mobility, so that uncovered interest parity holds.

v. The expected future exchange rate is assumed to be constant. As long as the expected future exchange rate changes less than one-for-one with the current exchange rate, this assumption does not affect the qualitative results of the chapter.

IV. Summary of the Material

1. Equilibrium in the Goods Market

Given that $NX=X(Y,\varepsilon)-\varepsilon Q(Y,\varepsilon)$, the goods market equilibrium condition can be written

$$Y=C(Y-T)+I(Y,r)+G+NX(Y,Y^*,\varepsilon)$$

In the short run, assume that P and P^* are fixed and (for convenience) equal to one, so that $E=\varepsilon$. Since P is fixed, assume that expected inflation is zero, so that $r=i$. Under these assumptions, goods market equilibrium can be rewritten

$$Y=C(Y-T)+I(Y,i)+G+NX(Y,Y^*,E) \tag{20.1}$$

2. Equilibrium in Financial Markets

Foreign currency is assumed to have no transactions value for domestic residents, so the choice between domestic money and bonds can be summarized by the LM relation,

$$M=YL(i) \tag{20.2}$$

which was introduced in Chapter 4.

Under the assumptions of perfect asset substitutability (*i.e.*, no risk premium) and perfect capital mobility, the choice between domestic and foreign bonds is captured by the uncovered interest parity condition:

$$i_t = i^*_t + (E^e_{t+1} - E_t)/E_t \qquad\qquad (20.3)$$

The chapter assumes that the expected future exchange rate is fixed at $\overline{E}$. Under this assumption, dropping time subscripts, uncovered interest parity can be rewritten as

$$E = \overline{E}/(1 + i - i^*) \qquad\qquad (20.4)$$

Given the expected exchange rate, when the home-foreign interest differential increases, home assets become more attractive and the home currency appreciates (E falls). In fact, the home currency will continue to appreciate until the expected depreciation (given $\overline{E}$) equals the interest differential, so that returns on home and foreign assets are equalized.

3. Putting Goods and Financial Markets Together

Substituting equation (20.3) into equation (20.1) gives the open-economy IS relation:

$$Y = C(Y-T) + I(Y,i) + G + NX(Y, Y^*, \overline{E}/(1+i-i^*)) \qquad\qquad (20.5)$$

The LM relation is given by equation (20.2). Graphically, the IS curve slopes down in Y-i space. An increase in the interest rate reduces investment, as in the closed economy, and in addition, causes the currency to appreciate, reducing net exports. Moreover, the position of the IS curve is affected by foreign output and the foreign interest rate.

4. The Effects of Policy in an Open Economy

The effects of an increase in government spending are depicted graphically in Figure 20.1. The left panel shows the IS-LM curves. The right panel plots the uncovered interest parity condition. An increase in government spending shifts the IS curve to the right. Output and the interest rate increase. Since the expected future exchange rate is fixed, uncovered interest parity (equation (20.4)) implies that the exchange rate appreciates (E falls). The increase in output and the appreciation of the exchange rate both work to reduce the trade balance. The effect on investment is ambiguous, because the output effect tends to increase investment, but the interest rate effect tends to reduce it.

A decrease in the money supply shifts the LM curve to the left. Output falls, the interest rate increases, and the exchange rate appreciates. Investment definitely falls, but the effect on the trade balance is ambiguous, because the fall in output tends to increase it, but the exchange rate appreciation tends to reduce it.

Figure 20.1: Expansionary Fiscal Policy in an Open Economy with Floating Exchange Rates

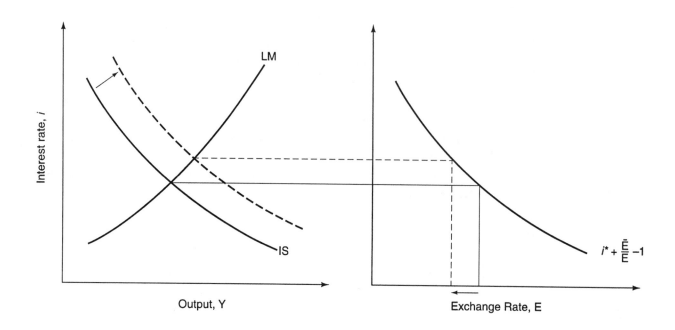

5. Fixed Exchange Rates

If policymakers fix the exchange rate (credibly) at $\bar{E}$, then expected depreciation is zero, and $i=i^*$ by uncovered interest parity. As a result, the IS and LM relations become

$$Y=C(Y\text{-}T)+I(Y,i^*)+G+NX(Y,Y^*,\bar{E})$$

$$M=YL(i^*)$$

Given fiscal policy, foreign output, and the foreign interest rate, output is fully determined by the fixed exchange rate and the IS curve. As a result, monetary policy is endogenous (*i.e.*, policymakers lose control over the money supply). Given Y, M must adjust to maintain i^*, in order to maintain the fixed exchange rate. If i ever strays from i^*, uncovered interest parity implies that the exchange rate will be expected to appreciate or depreciate. This is inconsistent with a fixed exchange rate.

Although policymakers lose control over monetary policy under fixed exchange rates, they retain control over fiscal policy. In fact, the effect of fiscal policy on output is magnified, relative to the case of flexible exchange rates. An increase in G would ordinarily lead to an increase in i. Under a fixed exchange rate, this is impossible. To maintain the fixed exchange rate, which requires $i=i^*$, the money supply must increase. As a result, an increase in G leads to an increase in the money supply as well. So the effect of fiscal policy on output is augmented by endogenous changes in the money supply.

V. Pedagogy

Confusion over the implications of the uncovered interest parity condition is likely to become an important issue in this chapter. If i falls below i^*, the home currency is expected to appreciate. So why does the home currency depreciate now? An analogy to the physical world is instructive. A roller coaster must rise before it can fall. Thus, if the exchange rate is expected to fall in the future (literally, E is expected to decline (appreciate)), it must rise now above its expected future value.

It is important to avoid any imprecision in terminology surrounding the exchange rate. Informally, one might easily describe a depreciating currency as a "falling" currency. This is inconsistent with the exchange rate convention that a decline in E means an appreciation of the home currency. It is probably wise to maintain this convention strictly in terms of language, as well as mathematics. Students have quite a lot of information and intuition to absorb in this chapter.

VI. Extensions

1. Fixed Exchange Rates and the Central Bank Balance Sheet

An appendix to the chapter discusses the central bank balance sheet and the management of fixed exchange rate regimes. It might be worthwhile to discuss this point in the main lecture to build intuition for the endogeneity of the money supply under a fixed exchange rate.

The asset side of the central bank balance sheet consists of domestic bonds plus foreign reserves. The liabilities side is high-powered money or the monetary base. The money supply is a multiple of the monetary base, as described in Chapter 5. Consider a monetary expansion in the form of a purchase of domestic bonds. This transaction creates high-powered money, since the central bank writes a check on itself. The monetary expansion tends to reduce the domestic interest rate. A fall in the domestic interest rate implies an expected appreciation to maintain uncovered interest parity. If the expected future exchange rate is fixed, an expected appreciation implies a depreciation of the current exchange rate, which is incompatible with a fixed exchange rate regime. To defend the exchange rate, the central bank must sell reserves to buy its currency. As reserves fall, the money supply falls. Ultimately, reserves fall by enough to offset completely the original monetary expansion. The fixed exchange rate and the IS curve determine output, which, together with the world interest rate, determines money demand. Since money demand is unaffected by the central bank purchase of bonds, the money supply cannot be affected either. In the end, the monetary expansion changes only the composition of central bank assets (more bonds, fewer reserves) and not the size of the money stock.

The amount of time required for the endogenous adjustment of the money supply depends on the degree of capital mobility. The model presented in the text assumes perfect capital mobility, which implies that the adjustment of the money supply happens instantaneously. If capital mobility is limited, the adjustment of the money supply will take more time. In these circumstances, the central bank will have some freedom to pursue independent monetary policy, at least temporarily. It may still lose reserves if it attempts an expansion, but it may be able to increase output for some period of time. Reasons for less than perfect capital mobility include a lack of developed financial markets in the home country, a reluctance on the part of international investors to substitute between home and foreign bonds, and capital controls—government-imposed limits on trade in assets with the rest of the world.

2. The Effects of Policy in Large versus Small Countries

Since small countries have larger shares of exports and imports in GDP than large ones, an exchange rate change is likely to generate a larger change in the trade balance relative to GDP in a small than in a large country. This implies that the IS curve is likely to be more sensitive to the interest rate—and thus flatter—for smaller countries, making monetary policy (under floating exchange rates) more effective in stimulating output in small countries.

Fiscal policy, on the other hand, is less effective in small countries, for two reasons. First, smaller countries are likely to have a larger marginal propensity to import out of income, which will tend to reduce the magnitude of the shift in the IS curve for a given size of fiscal stimulus. Second, since the IS curve is more sensitive to the interest rate, the increase in the interest rate (and the associated exchange rate appreciation) generated by a fiscal expansion will tend to have a larger (more negative) effect on the trade balance.

These results also hold under fixed exchange rates. Although the slope of the IS curve is irrelevant for the effects of fiscal policy (given $i = i^*$), it remains true that the horizontal shift of the IS curve will be smaller for a small country in response to a fiscal stimulus. Monetary policy is impossible *per se* under fixed exchange rates, but a devaluation will be more effective at stimulating output for a smaller economy, since the IS curve will be flatter.

3. Interdependencies

The chapter takes foreign income and the foreign interest rate as fixed. In fact, changes in policy in the home country can affect foreign income and the foreign interest rate. For example, an increase in government spending in the home economy tends to increase home output and cause a home appreciation. This implies an increase in foreign net exports, foreign output, and the foreign interest rate, effects that in turn affect the home economy. A full open-economy model would consider the effects of policy in the context of world equilibrium. A justification for ignoring effects on foreign output and the foreign interest rate is that the home economy is small, so that the changes in foreign variables are small, or that the effects on the home economy arising from changes in foreign variables are small compared to the direct effects. In any event, a full world equilibrium model with flexible exchange rates is beyond the scope of this text.

Matters are less complicated for fixed exchange rates, as suggested by a box in the text. Assuming that the strongest partner—call it the leader—in a fixed exchange rate system is free to set interest rates as it chooses, then the other members of the system must adjust. In this case, a monetary expansion in the leader implies a fall in the leader's interest rate and an increase in the leader's output. The increase in output implies an increase in net exports for other members of the system and a shift of their IS curves to the right. The other members must undertake monetary expansion to match their interest rates to the leader, *i.e.*, they must shift their LM curves to the right. The net result is an expansion in these economies. On the other hand, a fiscal expansion in the leader increases the interest rate and output in the leader's economy. The increase in output tends to shift the IS curve right in the other economies (through the effect on net exports), but the increase in the interest rate requires a monetary contraction in the other economies. Assuming that the interest effect dominates, the fiscal expansion in the leader's economy causes a recession in the other economies. For an example of these forces at work, see the box in the text on the effects of German reunification—which led to an increase in German demand and a monetary contraction in response—on other members of the European Monetary System.

VII. Observations

1. Conceptual Observations

The chapter assumes that the expected future exchange rate is fixed. A footnote points out that all of the qualitative results for this chapter hold as long as the expected exchange rate responds less than one-for-one to movements in the exchange rate. For example, if the expected exchange rate is given by

$$E^e = \lambda E + (1-\lambda)\,\overline{E} \tag{20.5}$$

where $\overline{E}$ is a constant, all of the qualitative results hold when λ is between 0 and 1. When $\lambda=1$, fiscal policy can longer affect output under floating exchange rates. An increase in government spending leads to an appreciation that fully crowds out net exports. The case where $\lambda=1$ is the canonical Mundell-Fleming model.

Chapter 21. Exchange Rates: Adjustments, Crises, and Regimes

I. Motivating Question

How Does the Exchange Rate Regime Affect Macroeconomic Adjustment?

Under fixed nominal exchange rates, there are two methods of adjustment: relatively slow, medium-run adjustment through the movement of prices and the real exchange rate, or faster adjustment through devaluation, often induced by a speculative attack on the currency. Under floating exchange rates, policymakers can use monetary policy to stimulate output during a recession. In choosing between exchange rate regimes, the apparently superior adjustment mechanism offered by floating exchange rates has to be weighed against the potential benefits offered by fixed exchange rates. The decision will depend on a country's specific circumstances.

II. Why the Answer Matters

The choice of exchange rate regime is a perennial and fundamental issue in international macroeconomics. Moreover, currency crisis remains a topical and intriguing phenomenon. This chapter provides students a basis to understand and think about these issues within the framework developed in the previous three chapters.

III. Key Tools, Concepts, and Assumptions

1. Tools and Concepts

i. Following Mundell, the chapter defines an **optimum currency area** as a group of countries that satisfy one of two conditions: similar economic shocks or high factor mobility within the group.

ii. An appendix to the chapter describes the **overshooting** phenomenon, whereby the initial effect of monetary policy on the exchange rate is greater than its ultimate effect.

IV. Summary of the Material

1. Fixed Exchange Rates and the Adjustment of the Real Exchange Rate

Suppose a country operates under a fixed exchange rate, $\overline{E}$. Perfect capital mobility implies that the home nominal interest rate equals the world nominal interest rate, *i.e.*, $i=i^*$. These assumptions imply that goods market equilibrium can be expressed as follows:

$$Y=C(Y-T)+I(Y,i-\pi^e)+G+NX(Y,Y^*,\overline{E}\,P^*/P) \tag{21.1}$$

To simplify, take expected inflation and foreign output as fixed. Then, equation (21.1) can be written

$$Y_t=Y(\overline{E}\,P^*/P_t,G,T) \tag{21.2}$$

This chapter focuses on the role of the real exchange rate ($\overline{E}\,P^*/P$) in equation (21.2). A real depreciation (an increase in the real exchange rate) increases output by increasing net exports. An increase in G would also increase output; an increase in T would reduce output.

Equation (21.2) specifies aggregate demand (AD). The time subscripts indicate that the home price level and home output can change over time. For convenience, the text assumes that G, T, and P^* are constant.

Aggregate supply (AS) is given by the same relationship derived previously, namely

$$P_t=P_{t-1}(1+\mu)F(1-Y_t/L,z) \tag{21.3}$$

Equation (21.3) incorporates the assumption that the expected price level equals the price level in the previous period.

The AS and AD curves are depicted in Figure 21.1. Note that the AD curve slopes down in output-price space, as in a closed economy, but for a different reason. In a closed economy, an increase in the price level tends to reduce the real money supply and, thus, to increase the interest rate and reduce output. In an open economy with fixed exchange rates, the interest rate is fixed at the world rate, but an increase in the price level causes a real appreciation, which tends to reduce net exports and output.

Now suppose that the economy starts from a position in which output is below its natural level (Y_n) and unemployment is above the natural rate. This scenario is depicted in Figure 21.1. If policymakers maintain a commitment to the fixed exchange rate, the relatively high unemployment rate will tend to drive down wages, prices, and expected prices and to shift the AS curve right until it intersects the AD curve at the natural level of output. Note that the increase in output along the AD curve results from the real depreciation created by the fall in the home price level. Although eventually the economy returns to the natural level of output, the process takes some time: output adjustment is limited by the speed of price adjustment.

If policymakers wanted to speed up adjustment, they could devalue the currency (increase the level of $\overline{E}$). A devaluation would create a real depreciation in the short run and shift the IS curve to the right. In principle, a devaluation of the right size could return the economy to its natural level of output almost immediately. In practice, however, the immediate effect of a devaluation will be to increase the price of imported goods, which has two implications. First, it will take time for a devaluation to improve the trade balance (the J-curve effect), and second, devaluation will lead to an immediate increase in the cost of living (since some goods are imported), which will tend to increase wages and slow down price adjustment. These effects suggest that devaluation will not eliminate adjustment and that it may be difficult to determine the size of the devaluation required to restore output to its natural level.

Figure 21.1: AD and AS in an Open Economy with a Fixed Exchange Rate

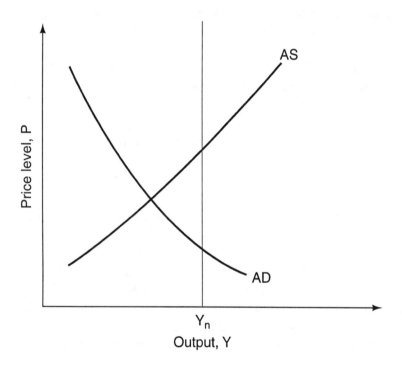

2. Exchange Rate Crises

The analysis in part I assumed that international investors believed that policymakers would maintain a fixed exchange rate of $\overline{E}$. In fact, as was demonstrated in part I, policymakers have the option of devaluing the currency or, in the extreme, abandoning fixed exchange rates altogether. If international investors believe a devaluation is possible, the expected future exchange rate will rise above the current exchange rate, and, by uncovered interest parity, the home interest rate will rise above the world rate by the amount of the expected devaluation (in percentage terms). Thus, in the face of an expected devaluation, policymakers will be required to raise the interest rate if they wish to maintain the fixed exchange rate. Since raising the interest rate reduces home output and increases home unemployment, policymakers may find this course too painful and may abandon the current fixed rate, either through a devaluation (which validates the original expectation) or by adopting a flexible exchange rate regime.

At times, international investors may have good reason to fear devaluation or abandonment of fixed exchange rates. A country's currency may be overvalued, implying that a real depreciation is necessary to improve output, the trade balance, or both. The quickest way to achieve a real depreciation is through a nominal depreciation. Likewise, a country may want to reduce its interest rate to get out of a recession. Fixed exchange rates preclude this option, but flexible exchange rates permit it through monetary expansion and concomitant nominal depreciation. The analysis above suggests, however, that an expected devaluation can trigger a crisis even if the initial fears of devaluation were groundless. In other words, there may be a self-fulfilling element to currency crises. Some economists attribute the Asian Crisis in part to self-fulfilling expectations.

3. *Choosing Between Exchange Rate Regimes*

Countries that operate under fixed exchange rates with one another are constrained to have the same interest rates. Thus, fixed exchange rates eliminate discretionary monetary policy and nominal depreciation as methods of adjustment during recession. In normal times, adjustment happens slowly—through price adjustment and changes in the real exchange rate over the medium run. In emergency situations, adjustment happens through devaluation, often forced on policymakers through currency crisis. Thus, the adjustment mechanism of fixed exchange rates does not appear terribly attractive.

On the other hand, as Robert Mundell pointed out in the 1960s, the loss of discretionary monetary policy is less important to the extent that countries operating under fixed exchange rates face one of two conditions: similar economic shocks or high factor mobility with one another. If countries face similar shocks, they would tend to choose the same monetary policies (and interest rates) even in the absence of fixed exchange rates. If countries have high factor mobility, movements of workers can substitute for real depreciation as a method of economic adjustment. In other words, workers will move from areas that require real depreciation to avoid high unemployment. A group of countries that satisfy one of Mundell's conditions is said to constitute an optimum currency area. As the name implies, it would make sense economically for such a group of countries to adopt a single currency. As the text argues, many economists believe that the countries of the Euro zone do not constitute an optimum currency area, since they satisfy neither of Mundell's conditions.

In some cases, the loss of policymaking flexibility under fixed exchange rates may also provide benefits. If countries have a reputation for undisciplined monetary policy, international investors may fear that a floating exchange rate system will allow too much latitude for inflationary policy. To the extent that such countries can commit to a fixed rate system, they eliminate the potential for discretionary monetary policy. Since a fixed exchange rate can always be abandoned, however, it is not always a simple matter to demonstrate commitment to a fixed rate system. One method is to enter into a common currency with a set of other countries, as Europe is doing at present. Another is to supplement fixed exchange rates with legislative or technical measures that prohibit (or limit) discretionary monetary policymaking. The latter arrangements—called currency boards—have become a popular policy tool in the 1990s.

Finally, the policy flexibility seemingly offered by floating exchange rates may be illusory. In practice, floating exchange rates vary greatly. Large and unpredictable movements in the nominal exchange rate make life more complicated for firms and consumers and have real effects in the short run since prices (and hence the real exchange rate) adjust slowly. Movements in the exchange rate are driven by expectations, which are not well understood. The model developed in Chapter 20 assumes a constant expected future exchange rate, which implies that the current exchange rate is determined by the current interest rate, a variable with a clear relationship to monetary policy. In fact, the expected future nominal exchange rate is not constant. The current nominal exchange rate depends not only on the current interest rate, but also on expected variables—domestic and foreign interest rates and the exchange rate—far into the future. Thus, the relationship between monetary policy and the nominal exchange rate is a bit more complicated than it seemed in Chapter 20. Moreover, to the extent that changes in the nominal exchange rate have real effects, monetary policymakers may be required to use policy to respond to unpredictable (and sometimes difficult to understand) movements in the nominal exchange rate. Thus, floating exchange rates do not allow policymakers complete independence; to some extent, policymakers are at the mercy of the foreign exchange market.

With this in mind, the choice of exchange rate regime requires weighing the potentially poor adjustment properties of fixed exchange rates against the costs of highly variable nominal exchange rates. The choice will depend on circumstances in each country—whether it is part of a group of countries that satisfy one of Mundell's two conditions, whether it needs to establish a reputation for monetary discipline, and so on.

V. Pedagogy

The discussion in this chapter is relatively sophisticated for students just coming to terms with open-economy macroeconomics. It is important to review carefully the adjustment mechanisms under fixed and floating exchange rates before tossing around terms cavalierly. (For example, clearly the present chapter of the Instructor's Manual is too sophisticated for students without some review.) It may also be helpful to discuss the role of the nominal exchange rate (under floating rates) as an automatic stabilizer. Under a fixed exchange rate, a shock to the goods market will affect output by the full amount of the horizontal shift of the IS curve (since the interest rate is fixed). Under a flexible rate, the same shock to the IS curve will have a smaller effect on output (since the interest rate and exchange rate can vary). In other words, flexible exchange rate systems tend to dampen IS shocks.

VI. Extensions

An appendix to the chapter introduces real interest parity (uncovered interest parity with real interest rates and exchange rates substituted for nominal interest rates and exchange rates) and extends it to a long-run relation, *i.e.,* a relation between the home-foreign long-run real interest rate differential and expected real depreciation over the long-run. The appendix then argues that trade (or more precisely the current account) must roughly balance over the long run. Thus, the expected long-run real exchange rate is that rate consistent with long-run trade balance. With this in mind, the current real exchange rate is influenced by two factors—the long-term real interest rate differential and the expected long-run real exchange rate. The text argues that movements in real interest rates explain most of the movements of the U.S. real exchange rate in the 1980s.

The appendix also presents a monetary policy example to demonstrate the overshooting phenomenon, whereby the immediate effect of monetary policy on the exchange rate is larger than the ultimate effect. The basic point can be grasped from the uncovered interest parity equation. Monetary expansion leads to depreciation of the nominal exchange rate and a reduction in the nominal interest rate. Under uncovered interest parity, a fall in the nominal interest rate implies expected appreciation of the currency. Thus, the initial depreciation of the exchange rate must be greater than its ultimate depreciation, so the currency can be expected to appreciate in the future. The appendix illustrates this point with a more sophisticated example, involving an announced sequence of interest rate reductions.

VII. Observations

1. Conceptual Observations

The real exchange rate drives adjustment in an open economy. In the short run, with prices fixed, movements in the nominal exchange rate create movements in the real exchange rate. Thus, in the short run, fixed exchange rate regimes have no avenue for adjustment, and shocks translate into changes in output. In the medium run, the real exchange rate can adjust through prices, and the flexibility of the nominal exchange rate is irrelevant.

Chapter 22. Pathologies I: High Unemployment

I.   Motivating Question

How Do Macroeconomists Account for Episodes of Prolonged High Unemployment?

The causes of the Great Depression can be explained within the context of the existing IS-LM model, augmented to account for bank failures and debt deflation. Explaining the course of the recovery is more problematic and seems to require a fuller description of the labor market. Likewise, the increase in European unemployment over the 1970s and 1980s can be explained by conventional macroeconomics: adverse aggregate supply shocks followed by tight aggregate demand policies. The explanation for continued high unemployment is the subject of strenuous debate.

II.   Why the Answer Matters

It would be troubling if macroeconomics could not say much about the most important economic event of the 20th century, the Great Depression, which led to the creation of the field. Moreover, analysis of the Great Depression may help economists understand the modern episode of high unemployment in Western Europe, which remains a pressing policy concern.

III. Key Tools, Concepts, and Assumptions

1. Tools and Concepts

i. The **New Deal** was a set of programs put in place by the Roosevelt administration to stimulate economic recovery during the Great Depression. The programs included, among others, **the Federal Deposit Insurance Corporation**, the **National Recovery Administration**, and **the National Industrial Recovery Act**.

ii. **Eurosclerosis** refers to the view that high European unemployment rates are the result of rigid labor market institutions. **Hysteresis** refers to the alternative view that prolonged high unemployment leads to increases in the natural rate of unemployment and, thus, that high European unemployment rates today are largely the result of tight aggregate demand policies.

IV. Summary of the Material

1. The Great Depression

The Great Depression affected many industrial countries simultaneously. In the United States, unemployment remained at extremely high levels for more than a decade. Output fell drastically from 1929 to 1933 and then grew at high rates through World War II. As Okun's law would suggest, however, many years of strong growth were required to reduce the high unemployment rate (25% in 1933) to normal levels. The unemployment rate was still nearly 10 percent in 1941.

Why did output decline so much? There are three elements to the explanation. First, the stock market crash in 1929 deepened an ongoing recession through its effects on consumer wealth and confidence. In other words, the IS curve shifted to the left. Second, the normal adjustment mechanism whereby a fall in prices would increase the real money supply (and shift the LM curve to the right) was thwarted by a collapse of the nominal money supply. The fall in output led to loan defaults and bank failures, which led to fears about bank deposits and to an increase in the desired currency-deposit ratio. As a result, the money multiplier decreased, and the nominal money supply fell (despite an increase in the monetary base) between 1929 and 1933. Cutting through the terminology, the normal process by which banks create money by lending part of their deposits collapsed because consumers were afraid to deposit funds in banks. As a result, the real money stock was more or less constant between 1929 and 1933, so there was no shift of the LM curve. Finally, deflation itself magnified the contraction in aggregate demand, as negative expected inflation led to high real interest rates, despite low nominal interest rates. In terms of the IS-LM diagram, if the nominal interest rate is on the vertical axis, a fall in expected inflation causes the IS curve to shift left.

What caused the recovery? One element is clear: after 1933, there was rapid growth in the monetary base. The contribution of the various components of the New Deal—the set of programs put in place by the Roosevelt administration to combat the Depression—is less clear. The creation of the Federal Deposit Insurance Corporation, which insured bank deposits, seems to have ended the banking crisis. Other parts of the New Deal may have improved expectations about the future by emphasizing the government's commitment to recovery.

The puzzle is why deflation stopped when the recovery began in 1933, despite the persistence of very high unemployment rates. One possibility is that the National Industrial Recovery Act (NIRA), enacted in 1933, succeeded in preventing firms from further reducing wages. Although there is evidence that the NIRA had an effect on wage setting, this hypothesis does not explain why deflation also stopped in countries without New Deal programs. Another possibility is that the combination of high growth and high unemployment created pressures for price increases through bottlenecks in production and increases in the cost of raw materials. Finally, prolonged high unemployment itself may have reduced the downward pressure of unemployment on wages. Some economists invoke the latter argument to explain the current economic situation in Europe.

2. Unemployment in Europe

The Western European experience seems to support the notion that prolonged high unemployment affects the relationship between inflation and unemployment. In the 1970s, Europe suffered increases in both inflation and unemployment, probably as a result of aggregate supply shocks. In the first half of the 1980s, inflation decreased while unemployment increased, probably as a result of tight aggregate demand policies. Inflation began increasing again in 1987, despite the fact that the unemployment rate remained at about 10%. This suggests the natural rate of unemployment was not far from 10%. In the 1990s, unemployment remained high, and inflation declined. By the end of the decade, inflation was decreasing slowly, suggesting that the natural rate of unemployment was below its current rate of about 10%.

Explanations for Europe's unemployment experience have centered on labor market institutions. This argument—the Eurosclerosis view—attributes high European unemployment (as compared to the United States) to its strong unions, high firing costs, and generous unemployment benefits. All of these factors tend to increase the natural rate of unemployment, either by increasing worker bargaining power or increasing nonwage labor costs (and hence the markup) directly. However, these features of the European labor market were already present in the 1960s and early 1970s and have weakened since then. Union power, for example, is declining. Some economists argue that labor market rigidities become more important during periods of greater structural change, when movement of workers across jobs is required. Thus, even though the institutions have not gotten worse on the surface, they have become more important because of changes in the economic environment. Simple measures do not suggest an increase in the pace of structural change in Europe over the past 30 years or so. One specific argument is that the decrease in the relative demand for unskilled labor has been accommodated by a relative decline in unskilled wages in the United States and by a relative increase in unskilled unemployment rates in Europe. This argument fits the evidence reasonably well for Europe as a whole, but does not do well for individual countries. In the United Kingdom, for example, relative unemployment rates for unskilled workers rose between the late 1970s and the early 1990s, despite a large fall in relative wages for the unskilled.

The weaknesses of the Eurosclerosis view have led some economists to consider an alternative, called hysteresis. Under this explanation, the natural rate of unemployment depends on the history of unemployment. When workers have been unemployed for a long time, they tend to lose skills and work habits and become less attractive to potential employers. In the extreme case, they become completely unemployable and have no effect on wage determination. As the long-term unemployed become less employable, a given unemployment rate has less effect on wage setting: for any given measured unemployment rate, workers tend to bargain for higher nominal wages. In other words, the wage-setting curve shifts up, and the natural rate of unemployment increases.

The hysteresis argument has two policy implications. First, disinflation may be more costly than was suggested in Chapter 9, because increases in the unemployment rate may have long-lasting effects. Second, in Europe, there may be scope for a reduction in the unemployment rate without a fundamental reorganization of the labor market, even if labor market reforms are desirable on other grounds.

Finally, recent research is exploring the possibility that hysteresis and Eurosclerosis may be complementary explanations of high European unemployment. In other words, the difference between European and U.S. institutions may explain why hysteresis has been more important in Europe than in the United States. As an example, suppose unemployment benefits last during an entire spell of unemployment in Europe, but only for a short time in the United States. If so, then the proportion of long-term unemployed in total unemployment will be higher in Europe, and hysteresis will tend to play a more important role in the economy's adjustment to adverse shocks.

3. Conclusion

The two major episodes of high unemployment in the 20th century defy a common characterization. High unemployment during the Great Depression was clearly triggered by an adverse aggregate demand shock. The causes of the current European unemployment problem are still under debate. Moreover, the rapid growth that absorbed unemployment in the United States after 1933 is nowhere in sight in Europe today.

One feature these episodes may share is the impact of prolonged high unemployment on the relationship between unemployment and inflation. Hysteresis may have prevented continued deflation in the United States during the 1930s and may be responsible for high unemployment rates in Europe today.

V. Pedagogy

The Great Depression is ancient history to today's undergraduates. To make the subject more compelling, instructors might consider introducing the material of this chapter with a discussion of Japan's current economic performance, and then taking up the Great Depression, pointing out the similarities between the two cases. A box in the text discusses the liquidity trap—the lower bound of zero on nominal interest rates—in the context of Japan's economic performance in the 1990s.

VI. Extensions

How would the disinflation exercise conducted in Chapter 9 be altered by the introduction of hysteresis? Recall that in order to reduce the rate of inflation from 14 to 4 percent over the course of five years, it was necessary to raise the unemployment rate from 6 percent (its natural rate) to 8 percent and keep it there for five years. The crucial element in this strategy was to preserve the gap of 2 percent between the unemployment rate and its natural rate. If the natural rate itself increases when the unemployment rate is high, then preserving this gap would require, not a stable unemployment rate, but one which increases over the course of the disinflation. Moreover, when inflation is again stabilized—at 4 percent—restoring the unemployment rate to its natural level implies a permanently higher rate of unemployment. Thus, the legacy of a prolonged disinflation is a permanently higher rate of unemployment. This is essentially the hysteresis explanation of high unemployment in Europe today.

VII. Observations

1. Conceptual Observations

Long periods of high unemployment are not inconsistent with the model constructed in the text, but the expectations-augmented Phillips curve implies that such periods should be accompanied by declining inflation. The Great Depression in the United States and the current experience of Western Europe seem to contradict this implication. Hysteresis reconciles the model to these facts by arguing that prolonged high unemployment tends to increase the natural rate of unemployment and, thus, to weakens the relationship between unemployment and inflation.

Chapter 23. Pathologies II: High Inflation

I. Motivating Question

How Do Macroeconomists Account for Episodes of High Inflation?

Historically, hyperinflations have always followed the same pattern: governments have budget deficits that they are unable or unwilling to finance without printing money, and the resulting high rate of money growth leads to inflation. The central role of money growth in creating hyperinflation is consistent with the macroeconomic model developed in previous chapters.

II. Why the Answer Matters

Hyperinflation tends to erode the basic economic mechanisms at work in market economies and can have political as well as economic implications. Two important episodes of hyperinflation occurred after the First and Second World Wars. In addition, a number of economies have suffered bouts of hyperinflation over the past thirty years, and Russia has struggled with high inflation since the liberalization of its economy, so the issue remains relevant today.

III. Key Tools, Concepts, and Assumptions

1. Tools and Concepts

i. **Hyperinflation** is very high inflation.

ii. **Seignorage** is revenue available to the government from the printing of money. The **inflation tax** is the loss in value of real money balances because of inflation. The inflation tax equals the inflation rate times real money balances.

iii. **Incomes policies** refers to some combination of wage controls or guidelines and price controls or guidelines. **Heterodox** programs to end a hyperinflation include incomes policies; **orthodox** programs do not.

IV. Summary of the Material

Hyperinflations are episodes of very high inflation. Typically, such episodes last less than two years. Historically, hyperinflations have always been accompanied by monetary expansions of an order of magnitude comparable to the inflation rate. A money-financed government budget deficit has been at the root of all hyperinflations.

1. Budget Deficits and Money Creation

The start of a hyperinflation is typically characterized by two circumstances: a social or economic upheaval that increases the budget deficit and an increasing unwillingness or inability of the government to finance its deficit by borrowing from the private sector. When these two circumstances coincide, the government effectively borrows from the central bank, which prints money to buy the bonds issued by the government. This process is called debt monetization. Under this scenario, money creation is given by

$$\Delta M/P = Deficit, \tag{23.1}$$

where *Deficit* is the government deficit measured in real terms. The LHS of equation (23.1) is called seignorage. It represents the revenue available to the government from the printing of money. It is convenient to express seignorage in terms of money growth and real money balances:

$$(\Delta M/P) = (\Delta M/M)(M/P) \tag{23.2}$$

2. Inflation and Real Money Balances

From the money-market equilibrium condition, equation (23.2) becomes

$$\Delta M/P = (\Delta M/M)YL(r + \pi^e) \tag{23.3}$$

During a hyperinflation, changes in actual and expected inflation are enormous relative to changes in output and the real interest rate. Thus, the evolution of L is dominated by the behavior of the inflation rate, which causes real money balances to decline sharply, even though the nominal money supply is rising very rapidly.

3. Deficits, Seignorage, and Inflation

If money growth is constant, Chapter 9 showed that actual and expected inflation eventually equal the rate of money growth. In this case, equation (23.3) can be written as

$$\Delta M/P = (\Delta M/M)YL(r + \Delta M/M) \tag{23.4}$$

Money growth creates inflation, which reduces the real value of money balances. Thus, money growth is said to impose an inflation tax: the tax rate is the rate of inflation (equal to $\Delta M/M$), and the tax base is the stock of real money balances (equal to $YL(r + \Delta M/M)$). The inflation tax generates seignorage for the government, because people need to increase their nominal money stocks in order to sustain their real money balances. Money growth has two effects on seignorage: on the one hand, an increase in money growth increases the tax rate, but on the other hand it reduces the tax base, as higher nominal interest rates cause people to shift away from holding money. Empirically, the relationship between inflation and seignorage is hump-shaped—at low inflation rates, seignorage increases with inflation; at higher rates, seignorage declines with inflation. Thus, there is some rate of money growth that maximizes seignorage.

In hyperinflations, money growth typically far exceeds the rate that maximizes seignorage. Why does this happen? In the long run, it is impossible for the government to raise more seignorage than the maximum possible under constant money growth. In the short run, however, the government can exploit the time it takes for real money demand to adjust to faster money growth and increase seignorage temporarily by increasing the rate of money growth. Over time, extracting seignorage in excess of the maximum under steady inflation requires *accelerating* money growth and *rising* inflation. Moreover, real tax revenues tend to decline with inflation (the so-called Tanzi-Olivera effect), because nominal tax collections occur with a lag. As a result, the real deficit (and thus the need for seignorage) increases over time, contributing to the monetary acceleration.

With respect to output, an increase in money growth initially increases output by increasing expected inflation and reducing the real interest rate. As inflation becomes very high, however, the monetary exchange system becomes very inefficient, prices carry less information because they change so often, and borrowing and lending is curtailed because of uncertainty about inflation (and hence about ex post real interest rates).

4. How Do Hyperinflations End?

Hyperinflations do not end naturally. Ending them requires the implementation of a stabilization program, which includes, at a minimum, a credible fiscal reform (reduced spending plus replacement of the inflation tax by ordinary taxes) and a commitment by the central bank not to monetize government debt. Orthodox stabilization programs rely solely on these two elements. Hetrodox stabilization programs add incomes policies (guidelines for wage and price setting) designed to coordinate the expectations of wage and price setters. Disinflation implemented during hyperinflation may actually be less costly (*i.e.*, have a lower sacrifice ratio) than disinflation implemented during a more moderate inflation, because high levels of inflation tend to eliminate inertia arising from the staggering of wage and price setting. When inflation is high, institutions change to allow wages and prices to adjust much more quickly. Still, inertia may persist if the stabilization program is not credible, and in this case, the associated output costs may make it difficult to sustain the stabilization effort.

V. Pedagogy

Instructors might wish to clarify two points. First, as noted in the text, there is a distinction between seignorage and the inflation tax revenue. Seignorage equals money growth times the real money supply. Inflation tax revenue equals the inflation rate times the real money supply. Under constant money growth, however, inflation will eventually equal money growth, so seignorage will equal inflation tax revenue.

Second, the chapter makes clear that hyperinflation has its roots in fiscal policy. So, as a qualification to Freedman's adage that "inflation is always and everywhere a monetary phenomenon," it is not always the case the inflation results from an independent decision of the central bank. Why does the central bank lend to a government that requires deficit finance? It may have no choice, because it is politically subordinate to the Treasury (or Finance Ministry), or it may do so because it fears the consequences of government default more than those of the high inflation that will result from debt monetization.

VI. Extensions

1. Government Solvency

Why would a government be unable to borrow to finance a budget deficit? Potential creditors do not have to lend to the government. They can earn a market rate of return by lending to the private sector. They will only lend to the government if the present value of expected repayment, calculated using the market rate of return, is at least as great as the amount lent.

The total repayments that the government makes to its creditors consist of interest payments plus amortization (repayment of principal) on the amounts borrowed. Where does the government get the resources to make these payments? The resources available to the government to pay its creditors consist of the primary surplus in the government's budget (the government's fiscal surplus exclusive of interest payments) plus the seignorage that the government can raise by printing money. Thus, for the government to be perceived as a good credit risk, the present value of its primary future surpluses plus seignorage must be expected to be at least as large as the debt that it has to repay. When this condition is met, the government is said to be solvent. Otherwise, it is insolvent.

Recall that seignorage is not unlimited. It reaches a maximum value even if governments are willing to tolerate very high rates of inflation. Thus, creditors will be willing to lend to the government only if they believe that the government will produce sufficiently large primary surpluses in the future to repay its debt.

2. Wage and Price Controls

Why do governments sometimes use wage and price controls in inflation stabilization programs? In the context of high inflation, the economy can be described by a long-run equilibrium in which the AD and AS curves are both shifting up over time at the rate π. The drift of the AD curve reflects monetary expansion; the drift of the AS curve reflects expectations-driven demand for higher nominal wages. As an extreme case of stabilization, consider a fiscal and monetary reform that eliminates monetary expansion. If such a program were implemented, the upward drift of the AD curve would stop immediately, but, under the maintained assumption that expected inflation equals lagged inflation, the AS curve would continue to shift vertically upward, reducing output. A freeze of wages and prices would eliminate the upward shift of the AS curve and the concomitant loss of output. Arguably, the elimination of the output loss would reduce the temptation of the government to abandon the stabilization program. Moreover, the immediate stabilization of inflation through the combination of monetary-fiscal discipline and wage and price controls might make the program more credible.

Why would stabilization programs not invariably feature wage and price controls? One reason is that it is difficult to implement them without freezing relative prices, which introduces costly microeconomic distortions. A second reason is that governments have often come to think of wage and price controls as substitutes for the fiscal and monetary measures that are the prerequisites for successful stabilization. Finally, a more subtle reason is that controls may themselves undermine the credibility of the stabilization program. If wage and price setters attribute the success of the program to the controls themselves, or interpret the imposition of controls as a signal that the government has a low tolerance for recession, they may question the government's commitment to the stabilization effort.

VII. Observations

1. Conceptual Observations

Governments do not have unlimited power to extract resources by printing money. There is a maximum level of seignorage associated with a constant rate of money growth, no matter how high that rate.

Chapter 24. Pathologies III: Transition in Eastern Europe and the Asian Crisis

I. Motivating Question

How Do Macroeconomists Account for the Post-Liberalization Collapse in Output in Eastern Europe and the Asian Crisis?

Eastern Europe's transition from central planning to a market economy required a huge reallocation of resources away from inefficient state-supported firms to new enterprises in the private sector. It has taken time for this reallocation to occur; in the interim, since it is easier to close down inefficient enterprises than to create new ones, output and employment have suffered. Moreover, the development of a market economy requires a state strong enough to enforce property rights, collect taxes, and resist ongoing pressure for subsidies to state enterprises. The development of the required governmental institutions also takes time. Without them, as is evident in Russia, the private sector cannot grow quickly enough to absorb resources made idle by the declining state sector.

Economists are still debating the causes of the Asian crisis. One view holds that the crisis was triggered by poor fundamentals—in this case, risky investments financed by foreign lending. An alternative view holds that the crisis was largely the result of self-fulfilling expectations—fears about the future of the economy that came true as a result of the sudden attempt by foreign investors to move funds out of Asia.

II. Why the Answer Matters

In addition to the human suffering during transition in Eastern Europe, the poor performance of Russia's economy since the collapse of communism may well have important political implications. Moreover, on the surface, the collapse in output during a period in which the economy should have become more efficient represents something of a challenge to the standard neoclassical model of macroeconomics. The Asian crisis is important in its own right, since it may have implications for the future economic performance of Asian economies, but also because it has created debate about how to prevent and manage future economic crises. Finally, in the context of the book, the analyses of transition and the Asian crisis draw on many of the tools developed in previous chapters.

III. Key Tools, Concepts, and Assumptions

1. Tools and Concepts

i. In a **centrally-planned** economy, the government (as opposed to the private sector) makes most important economic decisions, including establishing production plans and methods for individual firms and setting prices.

ii. **Price liberalization** is the elimination of government control over prices. **Privatization** is the transfer of state-owned firms to private owners.

iii. **Capital controls** refer to legal limits on the ability of domestic residents to borrow or lend abroad.

IV. Summary of the Material

1. Transition in Eastern Europe

Beginning with Poland in 1990s, the formerly centrally-planned economies of Eastern Europe have moved toward market based economies. Indeed, this transition extends beyond Eastern Europe. With the exception of Cuba and North Korea, all of the economies that were centrally planned in the 1980s are in some stage of transition away from central planning. The text focuses on the experience of five countries: The Czech Republic, Hungary, Poland, Russia, and Ukraine.

All of these countries have made substantial progress in price liberalization—the freeing of prices from the control of government planners—and have made at least some progress in privatization—the transfer of state-owned firms to private owners. Since privatization provides owners an incentive to maximize profits, and price liberalization allows prices to signal what firms should produce, these developments might have been expected to increase output. In fact, the initial transition period was marked by a dramatic decline in output (even after accounting for measurement error—which tends to overstate pre-liberalization output and understate post-liberalization output—in the official statistics). Moreover, despite very similar progress with respect to price liberalization and privatization, the five countries have fared differently over time. The Czech Republic, Hungary, and Poland have begun to grow, and measured GDP in these countries is near or (in the case of Poland) above its pre-liberalization level. Russia and the Ukraine are not growing, however, and GDP levels in these countries remain extremely low relative to pre-liberalization levels.

The basic explanation for the fall in output is the enormous reorganization of resources required to convert to a market economy. Liberalization created a substantial adverse supply shock and concomitant decline in labor demand for state firms. Demand shifted away from the products produced by state firms as a result of price liberalization, a decline in demand for defense-related goods, and the collapse of trading arrangements among centrally-planned economies, which led to a loss of export markets in Eastern Europe. In addition, many state firms simply did not know how to operate in a market economy. At the same time, lacking capital and expertise, it took time for new firms to arise in the private sector. Thus, although there was some increase in labor demand in the private sector (particularly in service sectors that required little capital), it was not sufficient to offset the fall in labor demand in the state sector.

Over time, the demand for labor in the private sector has increased in the Czech Republic, Hungary, and Poland, and some state firms have started to restructure, which will eventually add to labor demand. As a result, growth has begun. However, growth is constrained by a lack of domestic business expertise and the need for much more extensive restructuring before firms can increase production. Restructuring requires capital, initially creates a decrease in employment (since some plants must be closed and some workers must be laid off), and requires that someone in the firm have the authority and the incentive to make the needed changes. In many countries, privatization has not proceeded rapidly or effectively enough to create the incentives and corporate governance required to stimulate restructuring.

Russia and Ukraine have fared much worse than the central European economies. The text focuses on Russia, but argues that Ukraine faces similar problems. The main reason for Russia's poor economic performance is the inability or the unwillingness of the state to address two needed policy initiatives: the definition and enforcement of property rights and the elimination of transfers to state firms. With respect to the property rights, corruption, gangsterism, and the lack of contract enforcement have severely curtailed incentives to invest in Russia. With respect to transfers, even though official subsidies have declined, many firms have stopped paying taxes. As a result, firms have less incentive to restructure, since they can stay afloat by obtaining transfers—including tax arrears (unpaid taxes)—and the Russian government has a large deficit. It has been unable to finance this deficit with bonds; previous attempts to do so triggered an exchange rate crisis when it became clear that Russia could not repay at the required high rates of interest. Thus, with no immediate prospect of fiscal reform, Russia faces the prospect of monetary expansion (to cover the deficit) and hyperinflation. Since the needed policy measures require fundamental change in Russian institutions—formal and informal—they are likely to take some time (if they occur at all). Thus, Russia's prospects for fast growth in the near future are not bright.

2. The Asian Crisis

After years of high growth, Asian economies suffered currency crises in 1997 and deep recessions in 1998. There are two competing explanations for the crisis. The explanation based on fundamentals argues that high rates of growth in Asian economies prior to the crisis were sustained by high rates of investment, financed by borrowing from abroad. As Chapter 12 demonstrated, capital accumulation can increase growth temporarily, but not in the long run, because of diminishing marginal returns. As a result, growth was eventually going to slow down in Asia, and the high rates of investment could not be justified by reasonable expectations about future profits. Foreign investors were still willing to invest in Asia as long as they believed that the government would bail them out if their investments did not turn out well. Eventually, however, foreign investors decided that the government might not bail them out, evaluated the problems facing Asian economies, and decided to get out.

The explanation based on self-fulfilling explanations argues that foreign investors panicked and created an unnecessary crisis. A large fraction of foreign lending to Asia was short-term lending directly to banks. This created the potential for a dual run on banks and Asian currencies. When investors became nervous about Asia, they realized that the nature of bank operations (short-term borrowing and long-term lending) implied that banks could not repay all creditors at once, and that most Asian central banks did not have sufficient reserves to convert all short-term foreign lending into dollars at the existing fixed exchange rate. As a result, all foreign investors had an incentive to withdraw funds from Asian banks (*i.e.*, not roll over short-term loans) and convert them into dollars as quickly as possible, while funds were still available. When investors begin to withdraw funds from banks, they created a banking crisis; when they attempted to convert Asian currencies into dollars, they created a currency crisis, which eventually led to the adoption of floating exchange rates and a large depreciation of Asian currencies. The depreciation made things worse for Asian banks, since some of their borrowing was denominated in dollars. The dual run on banks and currencies created an economic crisis, which ended up validating the initial fears of foreign creditors.

Whatever the explanation for the Asian crisis, there is no doubt that it created a substantial recession in the affected economies. According to the open economy model presented in earlier chapters, the depreciation of Asian currencies should have stimulated exports and output. There are two reasons for the immediate recession in Asia. First, Asian governments tried to defend their fixed exchange rate parities with high interest rates for a time, before allowing their currencies to float. The high interest rates reduced investment. Second, the banking crisis left many banks bankrupt and unable to lend to firms, who were themselves suffering from exchange rate depreciation, since they had outstanding debts denominated in dollars.

The Asian crisis has generated debate over two issues. The first is whether capital controls—legal limits on the ability of domestic residents to borrow and lend abroad—have a place in modern open economies. Some point to the Asian crisis as evidence in favor of limiting short-term foreign borrowing. Others argue that, regardless of their desirability, such measures would be difficult to implement in practice.

The second issue is the appropriate role of the International Monetary Fund (IMF). During the crisis, the IMF played two roles: it helped countries design macroeconomic policies aimed at ending the crisis, and, conditional on the adoption of these policies, it lent funds to the countries to help them defend their exchange rates. Both roles have been criticized. Some have argued that the IMF recommended some inappropriate policies—increases in interest rates for countries in recession and fiscal contraction for countries with fiscal surpluses—and some irrelevant ones—various deregulation and reform measures. Some argue that the latter measures were an attempt by the IMF to use the crisis to impose a larger agenda on Asian economies. Moreover, some critics argue that the IMF should have lent more funds more quickly to Asian economies, while others argue that the IMF should not lend funds to countries in trouble. Those opposed to IMF lending believe that it should focus on coordinating debt restructuring (the conversion of short-term debt to long-term debt) by creditors and on negotiating agreements between a country and its creditors, in the event the country cannot repay in full.

3. Epilogue on Asia for the Instructor's Manual

At the time of this writing, Asian economies are beginning to grow. According to statistics printed in *The Economist*, as of the third quarter of 1999, Indonesia had GDP growth of 0.5% over the previous year, Korea 12.3%, Malaysia 8.1%, and Thailand 5.1%. These growth figures reflect, in part, the relatively low output levels in 1998. It remains an open question whether Asian economies will return to sustained rates of growth comparable to their experience before the crisis. Moreover, Malaysia, which adopted capital controls during the crisis and did not adopt an IMF program, has had a roughly similar experience to other Asian economies that maintained open capital markets and took IMF policy advice. Whether Malaysia's experience can offer any guidance about the possibilities or wisdom of capital controls, and indeed whether any of the policy measures suggested by the IMF or implemented in Asia had much to do with the speed and path of the recovery, remains open to debate.

V.   Pedagogy

The obvious way to freshen the lecture is to add information about current developments and relate them to the discussion of the text. These developments need not be limited to Eastern Europe and Asia. The Asian crisis, for example, has fostered a debate relevant to other countries. At the time of this writing, Ecuador has just announced its intention to adopt the dollar as its currency—in other words, to create the ultimate currency board. In the aftermath of the Asian crisis, there has been much debate about whether developing economies should adopt currency boards to prevent exchange rate crises.

VI.   Extensions

The first edition of the text contained a discussion of the economic performance of the Soviet Union. According to the best available statistics, over the period 1928 to 1987, average annual growth of output per worker in the Soviet Union was about 2.8%, compared to 2% over the same period in the United States. Growth slowed in the 1970s and 80s, however, as it did in the West. Growth was driven largely by a high rate of capital accumulation. As demonstrated in Chapter 12, however, capital accumulation cannot sustain growth indefinitely; eventually, the economy grows at the rate of technological progress. The Soviet Union achieved reasonably high rates of technological progress through the 1960s, but this came to a stop in the 1970s. Between 1970 and 1987, the rate of technological progress was essentially zero (in fact negative in the 1980s). The lack of technological progress and decreasing returns to capital together implied little prospect for future growth, hence the pressure for economic reform.

A question arises as to how the Soviet Union was able to generate technological progress for 40 years, despite the lack of incentives for individual firms to innovate. A possible answer is that technological progress arose from the adoption of new developments abroad. When such developments became too complex for central planning to replicate—arguably the case for the information technologies developed in the 1970s and 80s—technological progress ceased.

VII. Observations

1. Conceptual Observations

To function efficiently, market economies require a government strong enough, at a minimum, to define and enforce property rights, separate government from industrial finance, and collect tax revenue. Previous chapters assumed the existence of a government capable of carrying out these functions. Russia's experience illustrates the importance of these governmental functions and the potential difficulty in creating the institutions necessary to support market economies.

Chapter 25. Should Policymakers be Restrained?

I.   Motivating Question

Should External Limits be Imposed on Policymakers?

Possibly, but not because the effects of policy are uncertain. Policymakers understand that uncertainty provides an argument for moderation in setting policy and, to the extent they are benevolent, impose their own restraint. On the other hand, the strategic interactions between the private sector and the government and among political parties suggest that economic performance may improve when constraints are placed on discretionary policy. However, the need for discretionary policy in times of economic distress calls for care in the design of institutional limits on policymakers.

II.   Why the Answer Matters

Modern macroeconomics was founded on the premise that governments could take action to improve economic performance. Toward this end, the previous 24 chapters have discussed policies available to governments and the likely effects of such policies. Although caveats have been offered along the way, the basic message is that governments can take action to reduce economic fluctuations and increase the long-run level of the capital stock, but have little ability to influence growth, beyond establishing institutions that reward innovation. This chapter examines the limits on discretionary policy. It asks whether governments can be expected to exercise their discretion wisely and whether institutions can be designed to encourage good policymaking.

III.   Key Tools, Concepts, and Assumptions

1. Tools and Concepts

i. In economics, a **game** refers to strategic interactions among a set of players.

ii. A government faces a **time-inconsistency** problem when it has an incentive to deviate from a promised policy once private agents have made decisions based on the policy.

iii. A **political business cycle** occurs when policymakers try to generate expansions before elections in hopes of securing reelection.

IV. Summary of the Material

Despite the apparent beneficial role that macroeconomic policy can play, arguments for restraints on policymakers are common. These arguments fall into two classes: one view is that policymakers, in trying to do well, do more harm than good; another is that policymakers do what is best for them, rather than for society as a whole.

1. Uncertainty and Policy

One reason that policymakers may do harm is that the effects of policy are uncertain. A recent exercise at the Brookings Institution used twelve well-known world macroeconomic models to predict the effects of a specified monetary expansion. There was substantial variation in the quantitative results. Since such models capture existing quantitative knowledge about the effects of policy on the economy, the implication is that policymakers face substantial uncertainty about such effects.

If extreme macroeconomic outcomes are very harmful, uncertainty provides an argument for moderation in policymaking: the smaller the change in policy, the more narrow the range of possible outcomes. This argument is less relevant when the economy is suffering a severe recession or hyperinflation; in this case, the effects of relevant compensating policies—no matter how extreme—are likely to improve economic performance. There is every reason to believe that policymakers understand that uncertainty calls for restraint. Thus, the existence of uncertainty does not necessarily provide justification for imposing external constraints on policymakers.

2. Expectations and Policy

The relationship between the government and private sector can be described as a game, *i.e.*, in economic terms, strategic interactions among a set of players. Private firms and households make decisions based on expectations of future policy. The government forms policy based on the expected response of the private sector. Viewing the economy in this perspective can provide a rationale for external constraints on policymakers.

Sometimes a government has an incentive to deviate from a promised policy once private agents have made decisions based on the policy. In this case, the government's optimal policy is said to be time-inconsistent. For example, as discussed in Chapter 8, central banks can temporarily reduce unemployment below the natural rate by generating unexpected inflation. At the same time, if inflation is costly, central banks have an incentive to announce a policy of low money growth to reduce expected (and hence actual) inflation. Combining these objectives, the central bank's optimal policy is to announce a tight monetary policy to convince the private sector that inflation will be low, but to actually implement a looser policy to reduce unemployment (temporarily). If the central bank attempts to carry out this program, however, it will lose credibility quickly, and the private sector will set wages and prices in expectation of high inflation. This will eventually eliminate the ability of the central bank to reduce unemployment below the natural rate and at the same time contribute to high inflation. In the long run, the central bank's program will have no effect on unemployment (it will return to the natural rate) but will result in high inflation. Under these circumstances, economic performance would improve if the central bank could commit itself credibly to maintain low money growth. In this case, the public's expectations would be consistent with low inflation, and the natural rate could be achieved with a lower inflation rate. Thus, time inconsistency provides an argument for external restraints on government actions.

External restraints are needed because self-restraint may not be credible. However, care should be taken to preserve flexibility in times of economic distress. For example, one way to impose an external constraint on the central bank is to legislate a money growth rule. Such a restraint prevents the central bank from cheating on policy targets (a desirable outcome), but also eliminates its ability to respond to adverse shocks (an undesirable outcome). A superior alternative is make the central bank politically independent of the government in power and to appoint a central banker with a known distaste for inflation. The evidence suggests that central bank independence is associated with lower inflation.

3. Politics and Policy

Parts I and II assumed that policymakers were *benevolent*. In fact, politicians may act to maximize their own reelection prospects. If voters are shortsighted, politicians have an incentive to implement policies that generate short-run benefits, regardless of the long-run costs of these policies. There is not much evidence in favor of this proposition in the United States. Until the 1980s and aside from the Great Depression, the ratio of government debt to GDP tended to increase only during wars. In addition, the debt ratio has been declining since 1996. Thus, the shortsightedness of voters does not explain much of the evolution of deficits and debt. Moreover, if voters are shortsighted, politicians could improve their chances of reelection without much cost by generating expansions just before elections. Thus, there would be a political business cycle, with growth highest in the final years of presidential administrations. In the postwar period, U.S. growth has been highest in the final years of presidential administrations, but the difference across years has been relatively small on average.

Another source of harmful policies emerges out of strategic games among policymakers. Substantial policy disagreements occasionally result in wars of attrition between political parties that result in the postponement of needed policies, such as deficit reduction. Some economists believe that such problems warrant a balanced budget amendment to the U.S. Constitution. They worry about the effects of deficits on financial markets, and do not believe that Congress can either change fiscal policy in time to stabilize the economy or that it can impose fiscal discipline on itself. Most economists, however, believe that a balanced budget amendment has a cost—the elimination of fiscal policy as a macroeconomic policy instrument—that outweighs potential benefits.

V. Pedagogy

The discussion of time inconsistency provides an opportunity to revisit the issue of fixed exchange rates and exchange rate crises. A credible commitment to a fixed exchange rate eliminates a government's ability to conduct discretionary monetary expansion. Thus, it has been argued, a credibly fixed exchange rate will reduce inflation expectations and inflation. On the other hand, as numerous currency crises indicate, it is difficult for governments to convince markets that they will not devalue or adopt a floating rate in times of distress. Thus, there is an argument that some governments would do well to completely tie their hands with respect to monetary policy by establishing a currency board or adopting the U.S. dollar as their currency.

VI. Extensions

For students who know rudimentary calculus, instructors can present a simple formalization[1] of the time-inconsistency problem described in this chapter. Suppose the policymakers' loss function can be written as

$$L = (a/2)\pi^2 - b(\pi - \pi^e)$$

In words, policymakers care about inflation and unemployment in excess of the natural rate. The first term of the loss function reflects concern about inflation; the second term reflects concern about excess unemployment, which is determined by the difference between actual and expected inflation. If policymakers announce an intention to achieve zero inflation, and this is believed ($\pi^e = 0$), then they face two choices: they can either follow through on the announcement and produce zero inflation—in which case, $\pi = 0$, $u = u_n$, and $L = 0$—or they can act in a discretionary fashion, renege on their commitment, and attempt to achieve the socially optimal rate of inflation, conditional on $\pi^e = 0$. Minimizing L, subject to $\pi^e = 0$, generates an optimal rate of inflation of b/a. Implementing this inflation rate implies that $L = (-b^2/2a)$, which is smaller than the loss achieved by following the announced rule. The gain comes from the benefit of surprise inflation in lowering unemployment below the natural rate. Note that the form of the loss function implies that the cost of inflation is zero (at the margin) when inflation is zero, so there is always some gain to surprise inflation.

The problem is that the private sector is aware of these incentives. Therefore, in the absence of some credible mechanism that forces the policymakers to adhere to their announced policy, the private sector will never believe the announcement. Expecting that the policymakers will act in a discretionary fashion, the private sector will set $\pi^e = b/a$. Because this constant value of π^e does not alter the solution of the policymaker's optimization problem, the actual rate of inflation will indeed turn out to be $\pi = b/a$. However, since this inflation rate is no longer a surprise, there are no unemployment gains and the loss becomes $L = (b^2/2a)$, a worse outcome than would have been achieved by following the rule. Since

---

[1] The formalization is based on Barro, Robert J. and David B. Gordon (1983), "Rules, Discretion, and Reputation in a Model of Monetary Policy," *Journal of Monetary Economics*, 12:101-121.

policymakers are assumed to be benevolent—*i.e.*, their loss function accurately reflects social preferences—society would be better off by removing their discretion if possible.

VII. Observations

1. Empirical Observations

On average, the (postwar) growth rate during the second year of Democratic administrations is more than twice as high as the growth rate during the second year of Republican administrations. This fact is evidence in favor of the perception that Democrats place a higher weight on growth relative to price stability than do Republicans.

Chapter 26. Monetary Policy: A Summing Up.

I. Motivating Question

What Do Macroeconomists Know About Monetary Policy?

In the long run, monetary policy affects only the inflation rate. Thus, a central bank should adopt a target inflation rate, based on the costs and benefits of inflation. In the short run, however, monetary policy affects output, so the central bank must decide whether to deviate from its target to respond to economic shocks. Ultimately, this decision depends on the degree to which the central bank cares about fluctuations in unemployment and inflation. Operationally, central banks face the problem that monetary aggregates do not have a close relationship to inflation.

II. Why the Answer Matters

Whether the central bank should change interest rates is the preeminent macroeconomic policy issue. This chapter provides a basis to think about this question, in light of the long-run objectives of the central bank. Moreover, the United States is apparently in a golden era of monetary policymaking, often attributed to the talents of Alan Greenspan. Does the success of the Fed (or any central bank) depend upon the intelligence and luck of its leader, or can monetary policymaking be reduced to some relatively simple guidelines?

III. Key Tools, Concepts, and Assumptions

1. Tools and Concepts

i. The chapter introduces **monetary aggregates**. **M1** is the sum of currency and checkable deposits. **M2** is the sum of **M1**, money market mutual fund shares, money market deposit accounts, and time deposits.

ii. The **Taylor rule** argues that central banks should deviate from their target interest rates to the extent that they care about short-run fluctuations in inflation and unemployment.

iii. The chapter introduces terminology associated with the organization of the U.S. Federal Reserve.

IV. Summary of the Material

The analysis in previous chapters suggests that monetary policy has different effects in the short run and long run. In the short run, expansionary monetary policy lowers interest rates and causes the exchange rate to depreciate; as a result, output and the price level increase. In the long run, money growth determines inflation, but has no effect on output. Thus, the long-run inflation rate is determined by the long-run rate of growth of the money supply. With this in mind, the Federal Reserve has to choose a rate of inflation to target in the long run and to decide when and by how much to deviate from this target in the short run.

1. The Optimal Inflation Rate

The optimal long-run inflation rate depends on the costs and benefits of inflation. The costs of inflation vary with the level of inflation. At very high rates of inflation, money performs all of its functions badly: because its value changes often, it is a poor unit of account; because more money is required for transactions, it is a poor medium of exchange; and because its value drops continuously, it is a poor store of value. At low inflation rates, the costs of inflation are harder to identify. Economists emphasize three sources of cost:

i. Higher nominal interest rates cause people to economize on holdings of money. This effort requires resources, referred to as shoe leather costs.

ii. When the tax system is not indexed, the tax burden will depend on the rate of inflation. In the United States, this issue applies in particular to nominal interest income and capital gains. The tax distortions created by inflation affect the allocation of economic resources.

iii. Because higher inflation is associated with more variable inflation, nominal assets become riskier in real terms.

Inflation also has three benefits:

i. Seignorage—the amount of resources the government collects by printing money—increases at higher rates of inflation, at least over some initial range. However, the amount of seignorage available at low rates of inflation in countries with otherwise highly developed tax systems is too small to make this a powerful argument for low—as opposed to zero—rates of inflation.

ii. Since nominal interest rates cannot fall below zero, inflation makes it possible for governments to achieve negative real interest rates, and thus preserves the option to use monetary policy to stimulate output during recession.

iii. Money illusion may cause workers to resist nominal wage cuts, independent of the effects on the real wage. As a result, ongoing inflation may be necessary to achieve the real wage cuts that are sometimes required to reallocate labor across sectors.

2. The Design of Monetary Policy

Once a central bank has chosen a target rate of inflation, it must decide whether to set (and announce) a target for money growth (which it controls) or a target for inflation (which it does not control directly). In addition, the central bank must decide how much it is willing to deviate from the target in the short run to respond to economic shocks.

If the central bank decides to set a target for money growth, it must also decide what type of money to target. Money is not clearly defined. The United States defines several monetary aggregates. M1 is the sum currency and demand deposits. However, other assets, though not directly useable in transactions, can easily be converted into money. Such assets are said to be liquid. These include money market mutual funds, money market deposit accounts at banks, and time deposits. When added to M1, the sum of these liquid assets constitutes M2, or broad money. When the relative attractiveness of the assets in and outside of these aggregates (M1 or M2) change, the demand for the relevant aggregate will be affected. This happened in the United States when NOW (interest-bearing checking) accounts were introduced in the mid-1970s, as well as when money market funds and money market deposit accounts came along shortly thereafter. As a result of shifts in money demand, there is not a tight relationship in the United States between inflation and growth in either M1 or M2, although the relationship is closer for M2. In general, shifts in money demand make it difficult for central banks to achieve inflation goals by targeting monetary aggregates. Moreover, to the extent they desire to target M2, central banks face the additional problem that they cannot control M2 directly (they can control M1). The problems inherent in the use of monetary aggregates have led some central banks to shift to inflation targeting. Although central banks cannot control inflation directly, at least it is the variable they ultimately care about.

Given an inflation target, a central bank must decide when to relax the target to respond to short-run fluctuations. The Taylor rule argues that central banks should set short-term interest rates according to

$$i = i^* + a(\pi - \pi^*) - b(u - u_n)$$

where π^* is the target rate of inflation, i^* is the interest rate associated with this target, and u_n is the natural rate of unemployment. The coefficients a and b reflect how much the central bank cares about inflation versus unemployment. Basically, the Taylor rule says that the central bank should respond to short-run fluctuations to the extent it cares about them. Evidence suggests that the Taylor rule describes quite well the behavior of the Fed and the Bundesbank over the past 20 years.

3. The Fed in Action

The Fed is charged by the Humphrey-Hawkins Bill to promote both stable prices and maximum employment. Compared to most other central banks around the world, it has a substantial amount of political independence. Its organization consists of three parts:

i. Twelve Federal Reserve Districts, with a District Federal Reserve Bank in each.

ii. The Board of Governors, consisting of seven members, including the chairman, who are appointed by the President (and approved by the Senate) for 14-year terms. The chairman is appointed by the President from this group with a renewable term of 4 years.

iii. The Federal Open Market Committee, with twelve members consisting of the seven governors and five of the Reserve Bank presidents. This committee meets every six weeks and issues instructions to the Open Market Desk, which is in charge of open market operations—the purchase and sale of government bonds—in New York City.

In addition to open market operations, the Fed has two other policy instruments: changes in reserve requirements (the minimum amount of reserves that banks must hold in proportion to checkable deposits) and changes in the discount rate. Changes in reserve requirements have drastic effects on bank balance sheets and are rarely used. The discount rate is the rate at which banks can borrow from the Fed. Changes in the discount rate were once the primary instrument of Fed policy, but today this policy instrument has been superceded by open market operations and plays mainly a signaling role.

V.   Pedagogy

Some instructors may prefer to teach this lecture in reverse, starting from the institutional makeup of the United States Federal Reserve System, proceeding from there to problems of short-run monetary policy making, and then turning to the issue of the optimal long-run inflation rate. This sequence has the pedagogical advantage of moving from the more concrete to the more abstract. In addition, the observation that the Fed operates via target ranges for the growth rate of monetary aggregates makes it rather natural to ask why it does so—*i.e.*, why it announces any specific path at all, what determines the central tendency for the target path, and what determines the width of the band. Answering these questions not only provides a coherent framework for approaching the rest of the material in this chapter, but also presents an opportunity to link it with previous chapters, particularly with the general policy issues described in Chapter 25.

The announcement of a target range for money supply growth, for example, can be motivated as a form of precommitment, building on the material in Chapter 25. The Fed informs the private sector of what it intends to do, and in doing so puts its credibility on the line. Deviations from the announced policy will therefore impose a penalty on the Fed, unless it can provide a convincing rationale for the need to do so. Thus, making its intentions public should help the Fed to avoid the time-inconsistency problems of Chapter 25. The choice of the central tendency for the band can be explained as depending on the desired medium-term path of the inflation rate, which motivates the discussion of the optimal long-run inflation rate. Finally, the width of the band can be described as reflecting the outcome of a tradeoff between retaining the flexibility to respond to short-term shocks (including money demand shocks) and the desire to exercise restraint in the application of policy in view of the uncertainty discussed in Chapter 25.

A second possibility involves breaking up this chapter and integrating its various parts into the discussion of previous chapters. For example, as indicated in the Chapter 4 of the Instructor's Manual, the institutional material about the Federal Reserve System could be incorporated into the description of the money supply process. The existence of near-monies could also be integrated into the monetary policy discussion of Chapter 4 as a way of motivating money demand shocks. Finally, the discussion of the optimal rate of inflation could be incorporated into the discussion of disinflation in Chapter 9. As it stands, Chapter 9 discusses the unemployment costs of disinflation. Taking up the optimal rate of inflation in that context would facilitate a discussion of why a society might be willing to incur such costs.

VI. Extensions

As indicated earlier in the book, small open economies operating under fixed exchange rates do not possess monetary independence. Thus, for such economies, the issues of optimal long-run and short-run settings for monetary policy instruments concern the behavior of the exchange rate, rather than that of monetary aggregates. In the long run, the path of the exchange rate will determine the economy's inflation rate, in the same way that the rate of growth of a monetary aggregate such as M2 will determine the inflation rate in the United States. In the short run, policymakers will wish to retain the flexibility to adjust the exchange rate in response to changing economic circumstances. This is the role, for example, of devaluation, as discussed previously in the text.

There is also an exchange rate counterpart to the announced target ranges adopted by the Fed. Countries that operate under a fixed exchange rate often do not simply fix the rate, but adopt a predetermined central parity with a target range of variation around it. The central parity provides an anchor for the price level, and the band accommodates temporary deviations to permit the exchange rate to respond to shocks that might optimally require a devaluation or revaluation. The best-known example of such an arrangement is the exchange-rate mechanism (ERM) of the European Union—now defunct since Europe is on its way to a single currency. Target zones have also been adopted by several developing countries.

VII. Observations

1. Conceptual Observations

Target bands for monetary aggregates provide a compromise between the role of money as a nominal anchor and the retention of short-run flexibility to respond to shocks.

Chapter 27. Fiscal Policy: A Summing Up

I. Motivating Question

What Do Macroeconomists Know About Fiscal Policy?

Fiscal policy affects output in the short run—through its effect on aggregate demand—and in the long run—through its effect on investment. Fiscal policy is limited by the government budget constraint, which links the deficit to the increase in debt. Given the budget constraint, prudence suggests that governments should run fiscal surpluses during booms to balance deficits during recessions. Such policy allows the government to stimulate the economy during recession, but avoids the dangers inherent in accumulating a large debt.

II. Why the Answer Matters

The major long-term policy issue facing the U.S. economy is how to finance expenditures associated with the retirement of the baby boomers and continued aging of the population. This chapter alerts students to what lies ahead.

III. Key Tools, Concepts, and Assumptions

1. Tools and Concepts

i. The **inflation-adjusted deficit** is the deficit measure that omits the inflation component of interest payments on government debt. In other words, the inflation-adjusted deficit is the deficit measured in real terms.

ii. The **primary deficit** is government spending minus taxes.

iii. The **cyclically-adjusted deficit** measures what the deficit would be if output were at its natural level.

iv. **Ricardian equivalence** is the proposition that neither deficits nor debts have any effect on economic activity.

IV. Summary of the Material

In the short run, an increase in the deficit increases aggregate demand and real output, with the strength of the initial impact depending on expectations. In the long run, output returns to its natural level, but a higher deficit may affect the natural level of output through effects on investment.

1. The Government Budget Constraint

The inflation-adjusted deficit is defined as

$$Deficit = rB_{t-1} + G_t - T_t \qquad (27.1)$$

where all variables are expressed in real terms, B is real debt, and r is the real interest rate. The government budget constraint links the deficit to the increase in the debt. The constraint is given by

$$B_t - B_{t-1} = rB_{t-1} + G_t - T_t \qquad (27.2)$$

Defining the primary deficit as $G_t - T_t$, government debt can be expressed as

$$B_t = (1+r)B_{t-1} + Primary\ Deficit \qquad (27.3)$$

This relationship implies that, starting from zero debt and a zero primary deficit, a one-unit increase in the primary deficit for one period will generate a debt of

$$B_t = (1+r)^t$$

after t periods. To repay this debt after t periods, the government must run a primary surplus of $(1+r)^t$. If spending is unchanged, this means that a reduction in taxes today implies an increase in future taxes of equal present value. If instead of repaying the debt, the government merely seeks to stabilize it, it must run a primary surplus equal to the interest rate payment on the debt in every future period. This implies a zero inflation-adjusted deficit.

To examine the evolution of the debt-to-GDP ratio, rewrite the government budget constraint as

$$B_t/Y_t = (1+r)(Y_{t-1}/Y_t)(B_{t-1}/Y_{t-1}) + (G_t - T_t)/Y_t,$$

which can be approximated as

$$(B_t/Y_t) - (B_{t-1}/Y_{t-1}) = (r-g)(B_{t-1}/Y_{t-1}) + (G_t - T_t)/Y_t \qquad (27.4)$$

where g is the growth rate of output. Given some initial debt, equation (27.4) implies that the debt-to-GDP ratio will grow when there is a primary deficit and when the real interest rate exceeds the growth rate of output. To understand the latter effect, suppose the primary deficit is zero. Then, debt (the numerator) will grow at rate r and output (the denominator) will grow at rate g. The difference in growth rates is approximately the change in the debt-to-GDP ratio.

2. Four Issues in Fiscal Policy

i. Ricardian equivalence

Ricardian equivalence is the proposition that neither deficits nor debt affect economic activity. For example, given unchanged government spending, a tax cut today implies a tax increase of equal present value in the future. Therefore, consumer wealth is unchanged, and (according to Chapter 16's theory of the very foresighted consumer) private consumption is unaffected. An increase in today's government deficit will be matched with an equal increase in private saving. In practice, however, tax increases that are distant and uncertain are likely to be ignored by consumers, because they may not live to see them or because they do not think that far into the future. As a result, although expectations certainly affect economic behavior, it is unlikely that Ricardian equivalence holds in strict form.

ii. Deficits, output stabilization, and the cyclically-adjusted deficit

The fact that deficits reduce investment does not mean that they should be avoided at all times, but rather that deficits during recessions should be offset by surpluses during booms. In this way, fiscal policy will not lead to a steady increase in debt. The cyclically-adjusted deficit removes the effect of the business cycle from the deficit. Thus, it can be used to assess whether fiscal policy is consistent with no systematic increase in debt over time. Estimating the cyclically-adjusted deficit requires knowledge of two facts: the reduction in the deficit that would occur if output were to increase by 1% and the difference between current output and its natural level. The first fact is relatively easy to determine; as a rule of thumb, a 1 percent decrease in output increases the deficit by 0.5% of GDP. The deficit increases because most taxes are proportional to output, but most spending does not depend on output. The second fact is more difficult to ascertain, because the natural level of output depends on the natural rate of unemployment, which changes over time.

iii. Wars and deficits

There are two good reasons to run deficits during wars. First, deficits shift part of the burden of paying for a war to future generations (because they inherit a smaller capital stock). Second, by using debt instead of tax financing, the government avoids imposing very large and distortionary tax rates. Borrowing permits tax increases to be smoothed over time.

iv. The dangers of very high debt

High debt can lead to vicious circles. If financial investors begin to demand a higher risk premium to hold domestic bonds, the higher interest rate on government debt implies that the debt-to-GDP will increase unless the government increases the primary surplus. If the government does nothing, the increase in the debt ratio may lead investors to demand an even higher risk premium,

154

making the problem worse. On the other hand, if the government takes step to increase the primary surplus, it may create a recession, which will lead to a lower growth rate and (by equation (27.4)) faster growth of the debt-to-GDP ratio. In addition, the required fiscal measures may create political costs for the government and increase uncertainty about the political situation, which could increase the risk premium, thereby increasing the interest rate on government debt and compounding the problem. In short, the presence of a large debt leaves the government in a vulnerable position. Moreover, a vicious circle can be self-fulfilling: even initially unfounded fears that the government will repay its debt can lead to an increase in the risk premium, which will start the process in motion.

The problems associated with high debt lead some governments to consider debt repudiation. Although this can eliminate the problems of high debt in the short run, governments who repudiate debt may find it difficult to borrow in the future.

3. The U.S. Budget Deficit

The chapter concludes with an examination of the U.S. budget deficit. The bottom line is that budget projections look quite favorable for the next decade. Beginning in 2010, the retirement of the baby boomers and the rising cost of health care will combine to set off large increases in Social Security, Medicare, and Medicaid spending, which will create huge deficits in the absence of policy changes. The projections suggest that waiting to address policy changes until the budget moves to deficit will imply huge and distortionary tax increases in the future. Therefore, it makes sense to start making policy changes today.

V.   Pedagogy

Ricardian equivalence implies that the size of the deficit has no effect on economic activity, not that fiscal policy has no effect on economic activity. For example, starting from a position of budget balance, the balanced budget multiplier implies that an increase in government spending fully financed by taxes would increase aggregate demand and, thus, output. Ricardian equivalence implies that the effect will be the same regardless of whether the increase in government spending is financed by tax increases or debt.

VI. Observations

The difference between the official measure of the deficit and the inflation-adjusted measure is the rate of inflation times the outstanding government debt. For a given level of inflation, the higher the debt, the more inaccurate the official measure. Between 1968 and 1998, the official measure shows a U.S. budget deficit in ever year except 1969 and 1998. The inflation-adjusted measure, however, shows alternating deficits and surpluses until the late 1970s. Both measures show the deficit getting worse in the 1980s and improving in the mid-1990s. In the United States today, the difference between the official deficit and inflation-adjusted deficit is about 0.8% of GDP.

Chapter 28. Epilogue: The Story of Macroeconomics

I. Motivating Question

How Have the Core Ideas of Macroeconomics Developed?

Modern macroeconomics starts with Keynes. Since his *General Theory* appeared, there have been a series of challenges and counter challenges to his basic ideas, as interpreted by Hicks and Hansen. The core, as described in this book, is a collection of ideas that have survived these debates, and that help to make sense of the disagreements among economists.

II. Why the Answer Matters

Up to this point, the text has avoided describing economic research and ideas in terms of competing camps. Instead, it has provided a unified model, constructed on the basis of widely held views among macroeconomists, and emphasized the orderliness of economic research. This chapter provides students an overview of the tumultuous history of macroeconomic theory. It exposes them to the messier, dynamic aspect of research, and gives them some appreciation of how quickly economic orthodoxy can and has changed.

III. Key Tools, Concepts, and Assumptions

1. Tools and Concepts

The chapter introduces some terms associated with the intellectual history of macroeconomics. Such terms include, among others, the **neoclassical synthesis**, **Keynesians**, **monetarists**, **new classicals**, and **new Keynesians**.

IV. Summary of the Material

1. Keynes and the Great Depression

Few economists during the 1930s could provide a coherent explanation for the depth and breadth of the Great Depression. Keynes' *General Theory* delivered an intellectual framework to explain events and guide policy. Keynes emphasized aggregate demand; in particular, the slow adjustment back to the natural level of output after an adverse demand shock.

2. The Neoclassical Synthesis

By the early 1950s, a consensus had emerged around an interpretation of Keynes' ideas in the form of the IS-LM model, developed by Hicks and Hansen. This "neoclassical synthesis," as Samuelson called it, omitted the role of expectations and wage-price adjustment. During this period, Modigliani and Friedman developed the theory of consumption, Tobin developed the theory of investment (which was further developed and tested by Jorgensen), and Tobin also developed the theory of money demand and, more generally, portfolio selection. These developments were embodied in large macroeconomic models, pioneered by Klein. At the same time and independently, Solow developed growth theory.

The dissent from the mainstream consensus at this time was represented by monetarists, led by Friedman, who questioned both that governments wanted to do good macroeconomically, and that they actually knew enough to succeed. The debate between Keynesians and monetarists centered on three issues:

i. Monetary versus fiscal policy

Monetarists questioned the emphasis of the early Keynesians on the power of fiscal policy to stabilize output. Instead, monetarists emphasized the power of monetary policy to destabilize the economy unless the Fed were constrained by a monetary growth rule.

ii. The nature of the Phillips curve

Keynesians believed that the Phillips curve offered a permanent long-run tradeoff between inflation and unemployment. Friedman and Phelps argued that the tradeoff would disappear if policymakers tried to exploit it.

iii. The role of policy

Keynesians believed that fiscal and monetary policy could be used to fine tune macroeconomic performance to avoid fluctuations. Monetarists argued instead that economists did not know enough to stabilize output and that, in any event, policymakers could not be trusted to do the right thing. They should therefore be bound by simple rules.

3. The Rational Expectations Critique

The mainstream consensus of the 1960s received two challenges in the 1970s. The first challenge was empirical. Aggregate demand shocks could not account for stagflation—simultaneous increases in inflation and unemployment—which arose during the 1970s. The second challenge was intellectual. The new rational expectations view argued that people form expectations about the future using all available information, including economic theory and econometric models, rather than solely on the basis of the past behavior of the variables they are trying to forecast. This idea posed three challenges for Keynesian macroeconomics:

i. The Lucas critique

Existing macroeconomic models depicted behavioral variables dependent on expectations as functions of current and lagged values of other variables in the model. Under rational expectations, there was no reason to suppose that these historical relationships would not change if the policy regime changed. Thus, such models were effectively useless for analyzing the consequences of changes in policy, which was one of the primary purposes for which they were created.

ii. Rational expectations and the Phillips curve

The existing Keynesian models associated deviations of output from its equilibrium level with incorrect expectations of inflation, and slow adjustment to the natural level of output was an outcome of the slow adjustment of expectations. When rational expectations were introduced into these models, the absence of systematic forecasting errors meant that only unexpected shocks could cause output to deviate from its natural rate. Moreover, such deviations would last only as long as existing nominal wage contracts that had failed to anticipate the shock.

iii. Optimal control versus game theory

Under rational expectations, policy formulation affects the expectations formed by the private sector. Thus, the policy problem should not be characterized as an optimal control problem, but rather as a strategic game between policymakers and the private sector. Game theory led to different implications for policy. For example, the time inconsistency problem (discussed in Chapter 25) implied that discretion on the part of benevolent policymakers could lead to worse outcomes than rules.

In sum, rational expectations implied that Keynesian models could not be used to evaluate potential policy measures, that Keynesian models could not explain long-lasting deviations of output from its natural level, and that the theory of policy needed to be redesigned, using the tools of game theory.

Rational expectations quickly became the accepted working assumption in macroeconomics, and theories of economic behavior in goods, financial, and labor markets began to be reevaluated in light of this modification. Hall's random walk of consumption result and the Dornbusch overshooting model were two early successes. In addition, Fischer and Taylor showed that the staggering of wage and price decisions could imply long-lasting deviations of output from its natural level even under rational expectations. This finding resolved one of the issues raised by the rational expectations critique. Finally, research on policy games led to a new emphasis on (and more rigorous thinking about) credibility and commitment on the part of policymakers.

4. Current Developments

At present, macroeconomic researchers tend to cluster into three groups: new classicals, new Keynesians, and new growth theorists.

The research agenda of the new classicals consists of an attempt to explain macroeconomic fluctuations as the outcome of shocks to competitive markets with fully flexible wages and prices. These models assume that output is always at its natural level, and interpret fluctuations as arising from movements in the natural level, triggered by technological changes. The problem with this view is that the nature of technological progress does not seem consistent with the types of output fluctuations typically associated with business cycles. Moreover, there is strong evidence that money affects output.

New Keynesians essentially accept the synthesis that has emerged in response to the rational expectations critique, and their research agenda consists of exploring the implications of market imperfections for macroeconomic behavior. Research covers areas such as efficiency wages, imperfections in credit markets, and sources of nominal rigidities.

Finally, new growth theory is in the process of reexamining the neoclassical growth model to understand the determinants of productivity growth, as well as the potential role of increasing returns to scale.

5. The Core

Most macroeconomists would agree on the following propositions:

i. In the short run, shifts in aggregate demand affect output.

ii. In the medium run, output returns to its natural level.

iii. In the long run, the evolution of the level of output is determined by capital accumulation and technological progress.

iv. Monetary policy affects output in the short run, but not in the medium or long run. A higher rate of money growth eventually translates one-for-one into a higher rate of inflation.

v. Fiscal policy has short-run, medium-run, and long-run effects on output. Larger deficits tend to increase output in the short run, but to decrease capital accumulation and output in the long run.

Major areas of disagreement concern the length of the short run and the role for policy.

V. Pedagogy

This is the first chapter of the book that recognizes explicitly sources of disagreement among economists. The book has presented a unified model built around a core of widely held beliefs. Implicit in this presentation, and in the concluding comments of the chapter, is the suggestion that future progress will likely arise out of the core. On the other hand, a reading of the intellectual history described in this chapter suggests that progress may well overturn part of the core (which part, of course, is unknown) or at least lead to a reinterpretation of some part of the core. The major developments in macroeconomic theory have been revolutions of a sort, with new syntheses cobbled together afterwards to make sense of competing theories. Students may not want to rule out the possibility that new research will challenge parts of the core.

Answers to End-of-Chapter
Questions and Problems

Chapter 1

1. a. True.
    b. True.
    c. False.
    d. True.
    e. False.
    f. False.

2. a.

	1960-98	1997-99
US	3.1%	3.8%
EU	3.1%	2.5%
Japan	5.8%	-1.0%

While the US growth rate higher than its long-run average over the period, the growth rate has slowed relative to long-run averages in both the EU and Japan over the last few years.

   b. Sometimes the economy is growing quickly, other times it is growing slowly or even contracting. The last few years of rapid growth in the US do not imply that the long-run average rate of growth has increased back to its pre-1974 level.

3. a. The data in the web page are:

Real Gross Domestic Product,
Real Final Sales of Domestic Product, and
Real Gross National Product, Quarterly, 1959-96
[Percent change from preceding quarter]

	Gross domestic product	Final sales of domestic product	Gross national product
1959: I	8.6	9.2	8.6
II	11.2	7.3	11.1
III	-0.3	5.3	-0.2
IV	1.7	-1.3	1.9
1996: I	1.8	2.6	1.8
II	6.0	5.2	5.7
III	1.0	0.2	0.6
IV	4.3	4.5	4.9

suggesting that recessions typically last two-three quarters and that the most severe recessions in that period were the recessions of 1974-75 and 1981-82.

b. Percentage Changes in:

	Output Growth	Inflation
1968:	4.7	4.4
I	7.5	4.7
II	7.1	4.1
III	3.0	3.8
IV	1.8	5.5
1969:	3.0	4.7
I	6.2	3.8
II	1.0	5.0
III	2.3	5.8
IV	-2.0	5.1
1970:	0.1	5.3
I	-0.7	6.0
II	0.6	5.7
III	3.7	3.4
IV	-3.9	5.4
1971:	3.3	5.2
I	11.3	6.4
II	2.3	5.5
III	2.6	4.4
IV	1.1	3.3

If history simply repeats itself, the United States might have a short recession (lasting perhaps one year) accompanied by an acceleration in the rate of inflation by about one percentage point.

4. a. Banking services, business services.

b. Not only has the relative demand for skilled workers increased but the industries where this effect is the strongest are making up a greater fraction of the economy.

5. 1. Low unemployment might lead to an increase in inflation.

2. Although measurement error certainly contributes to the measured slowdown in growth, there are other issues to consider as well, including the productivity of new research and accumulation of new capital.

3. Although labor market rigidities may be important, it is also important to consider that these rigidities may not be excessive, and that high unemployment may arise from flawed macroeconomic policies.

4. Although there were serious problems with regard to the management of Asian financial systems, it is important to consider the possibility that the flight of foreign capital from these

countries worsened the situation by causing a severe stock market crash and exchange rate depreciation.

5. Although the Euro will remove obstacles to free trade between European countries, each country will be forced to give up its own monetary policy.

* 6. a. From Chapter 1: US output 1997=$8b; China output 1996=$.84b. Note that China's output in 1997 is $(.84)*(1.09) b. Equating output for some time t in the future:

$8*(1.03)^t=(.84*1.09)*(1.09)^t$
$8/(.84*1.09)=(1.09/1.03)^t$
$8.737=(1.058)^t$
$t =\ln(8.737)/\ln(1.058) \approx 38\text{yrs}$

b. From Chapter 1: US output/worker in 1997=$29,800; China output/per worker in 1996=$700

$29.8*(1.03)^t=(.7*1.09)*(1.09)^t$
$t\approx 65$ years

Chapter 2

1. a. False.
   b. Uncertain: real or nominal GDP.
   c. True.
   d. True.
   e. False. The level of the CPI means nothing. Its rate of change tells us about inflation.
   f. Uncertain. Which index is better depends on what we are trying to measure—inflation faced by consumers or by the economy as a whole.

2. a. +$100; Personal Consumption Expenditures
   b. no change: intermediate good
   c. +$200 million; Gross Private Domestic Fixed Investment
   d. +$200 million; Net Exports
   e. no change: the jet was already counted when it was produced, *i.e.*, presumably when Delta (or some other airline) bought it new as an investment.

*3. a. Measured GDP increases by $10+$12=$22.
   b. True GDP should increase by much less than $22 because by working for an extra hour, you are no longer producing the work of cooking within the house. Since cooking within the house is a final service, it should count as part of GDP. Unfortunately, it is hard to measure the value of work within the home, which is why measured GDP does not include it.

4. a. $1,000,000 the value of the silver necklaces.

   b. 1st Stage: $300,000. 2nd Stage: $1,000,00-$300,000=$700,000.
   GDP: $300,000+$700,000=$1,000,000.

   c. Wages: $200,000 + $250,000=$450,000.
   Profits: ($300,000-$200,000)+($1,000,000-$250,000-300,000)
             =$100,000+$450,000=$550,000.
   GDP: $450,000+$550,000=$1,000,000.

5. a. 1998 GDP: 10*$2,000+4*$1,000+1000*$1=$25,000
   1999 GDP: 12*$3,000+6*$500+1000*$1=$40,000
   Nominal GDP has increased by 60%.

   b. 1998 real (1998) GDP: $25,000
   1999 real (1998) GDP: 12*$2,000+6*$1,000+1000*$1=$31,000
   Real (1998) GDP has increased by 24%.

   c. 1998 real (1999) GDP: 10*$3,000+4*$500+1,000*$1=$33,000
   1999 real (1999) GDP: $40,000.
   Real (1999) GDP has increased by 21.2%.

   d. True.

166

6. a. 1998 base year:
    Deflator(1998)=1; Deflator(1999)=$40,000/$31,000=1.29
    Inflation=29%

    b. 1999 base year:
    Deflator(1998)=$25,000/$33,000=0.76; Deflator(1999)=1
    Inflation=(1-0.76)/0.76=.32=32%

    c. Yes

7. a. 1998 real GDP = 10*$2,500 + 4*$750 + 1000*$1 = $29,000
        1999 real GDP = 12*$2,500 + 6*$750 + 1000*$1 = $35,500

    b. (35,500-29,000)/29,000 = .224 = 22.4%

    c. Deflator in 1998=$25,000/$29,000=.86
       Deflator in 1999=$40,000/$35,500=1.13
       Inflation = (1.13 -.86)/.86 = .314 = 31.4%.

8. a. The quality of a routine checkup improves over time. Checkups now may include EKGs, for example. Medical services are particularly affected by this problem due to constant improvements in medical technology.

    b. You need to know how the market values pregnancy checkups with and without ultra-sounds in that year.

    c. This information is not available since all doctors adopted the new technology simultaneously. Still, you can tell that the quality adjusted increase will be lower than 20%.

*9. a. approximately 2.5%

    b. 1992 real GDP growth: 2.7%;
    unemployment rate Jan 92: 7.3%; unemployment rate Jan 93: 7.3%
    Supports Okun's law because the unemployment rate does not change when the growth rate of real GDP is near 2.5%

    c. -2 percentage points change in the unemployment rate; 5 percent GDP growth

    d. The growth rate of GDP must increase by 2.5 percentage points.

Chapter 3

1. a. True.
    b. False. Government spending was 18% if GDP without transfers.
    c. False. The propensity to consume must be less than one for our model to be well defined.
    d. True.
    e. False.
    f. False. The increase in output is one times the multiplier.

2. a. $Y=160+0.6*(Y-100)+150+150$
        $0.4Y=460-60$
        $Y=1000$

    b. $Y_D=Y-T=1000-100=900$

    c. $C=160+0.6*(900)=700$

3. a. No. The goods market is not in equilibrium. From part 2a,
        Demand$=1000=C+I+G=700+150+150$

    b. Yes. The goods market is in equilibrium.

    c. No. Private saving$=Y-C-T=200$. Public saving $=T-G=-50$. National saving (or in short, saving) equals private plus public saving, or 150. National saving equals investment.

4. a. Roughly consistent. $C/Y=700/1000=70\%$; $I/Y=G/Y=150/1000=15\%$.

    b. Approximately -2%.

    c. Y needs to fall by 2%, or from 1000 to 980. The parameter c_0 needs to fall by 20/multiplier, or by $20*(.4)=8$. So c_0 needs to fall from 160 to 152.

    d. The change in c_0 (-8) is less than the change in GDP (-20) due to the multiplier.

5. a. Y increases by $1/(1-c_1)$

    b. Y decreases by $c_1/(1-c_1)$

    c. The answers differ because spending affects demand directly, but taxes affect demand through consumption, and the propensity to consume is less than one.

    d. The change in Y equals $1/(1-c_1) - c_1/(1-c_1) = 1$. Balanced budget changes in G and T are not macroeconomically neutral.

    e. The propensity to consume has no effect because the balanced budget tax increase aborts the multiplier process. Y and T both increase by on unit, so disposable income, and hence consumption, do not change.

*6. a. The tax rate is less than one.

b. $Y=c_0+c_1Y_D+I+G$ implies
$Y=[1/(1-c_1+c_1t_1)]*[c_0-c_1t_0+I+G]$

c. The multiplier $= 1/(1-c_1+c_1t_1) <1/(1- c_1)$, so the economy responds less to changes in autonomous spending when t_1 is positive.

d. Because of the automatic effect of taxes on the economy, the economy responds less to changes in autonomous spending than in the case where taxes are independent of income. So output tends to vary less, and fiscal policy is called an automatic stabilizer.

*7. a. $Y=[1/(1-c_1+c_1t_1)]*[c_0-c_1t_0+I+G]$

b. $T = c_1t_0 + t_1*[1/(1-c_1+c_1t_1)]*[c_0-c_1t_0+I+G]$

c. Both Y and T decrease.

d. If G is cut, Y decreases even more.

Chapter 4

1. a. True.
    b. False.
    c. True.
    d. True.
    e. False.
    f. False.
    g. True.

2. a. i=0.05: Money demand = $18,000; Bond demand = $32,000
    i=.1:   Money demand = $15,000; Bond demand = $35,000
    b. Money demand decreases when the interest rate increases; bond demand increases. This is consistent with the text.
    c. The demand for money falls by 50%.
    d. The demand for money falls by 50%.
    e. A 1% increase (decrease) in income leads to a 1% increase (decrease) in money demand. This effect is independent of the interest rate.

3. a. $i=100/\$P_B - 1$; i=33%; 18%; 5% when $\$P_B$ =$75; $85; $95.
    b. Negative.
    c. $\$P_B = 100/(1.08) \approx \$93$

4. a. $\$20 = M^D = \$100*(.25 - i)$
    i=5%

    b. $M = \$100*(.25 - .15)$
    M=$10

5. a. $B^D = 50,000 - 60,000 (.35 - i)$
    An increase in the interest rate of 10% increases bond demand $6,000.

    b. An increase in wealth increases bond demand, but has no effect on money demand.

    c. An increase in income increases money demand, but decreases bond demand.

    d. When people earn more income, this does not change their wealth right away. Thus, they increase their demand for money and decrease their demand for bonds.

6. a. Demand for high-powered money=0.1*$Y*(.8-4i)

    b. $100 b = 0.1*$5,000b*(.8-4i)
    i=15%

    c. M=(1/.1)*$100 b=$1,000 b
    M= M^d at the interest derived in part b.

6. d. If H increases to $300, falls to 5%.

   e. M=(1/.1)*$300 b=$3,000 b

7. a. $16 is withdrawn on each trip to the bank.
   Money holdings—day one: $16; day two: $12; day three: $8; day four: $4.

   b. Average money holdings are $10.

   c. $8 dollar withdrawals; money holdings of $8; $4; $8; $4.

   d. Average money holdings are $6.

   e. $16 dollar withdrawals; money holdings of $0; $0; $0; $16.

   f. Average money holdings are $4.

   g. Based on these answers, ATMs and credit cards have reduced money demand.

8. a. velocity=1/(M/$Y)=1/L(i)
   b. Velocity roughly doubled between the mid 1960s and the mid 1990s.
   c. ATMS and credit cards reduced L(i) so velocity increased.

Chapter 5

1. a. True.
   b. True.
   c. False.
   d. False. The balanced budget multiplier is positive (it equals one), so the IS curve shifts right.
   e. False.
   f. Uncertain. An increase in G leads to an increase in Y (which tends to increase investment), but an increase in the interest rate (which tends to reduce investment).
   g. True.

*2. Firms deciding how to use their own funds will compare the return on bonds to the return on investment. When the interest rate on bonds increases, they become more attractive, and firms are more likely to use their funds to purchase bonds, rather than to finance investment projects.

3. a. $Y=[1/(1-c_1)]*[c_0-c_1T+I+G]$
   The multiplier is $1/(1-c_1)$.

   b. $Y=[1/(1-c_1-b_1)]*[c_0-c_1T+ b_0-b_2i +G]$
   The multiplier is $1/(1-c_1-b_1)$. Since the multiplier is larger than the multiplier in part a, the effect of a change in autonomous spending is bigger than in part a.

   c. Substituting for the interest rate in the answer to part b:
   $Y=[1/(1-c_1-b_1+ b_2d_1/d_2)]*[c_0-c_1T+ b_0+(b_2*M/P)/d_2 +G]$
   The multiplier is $1/(1-c_1-b_1+ b_2d_1/d_2)$.

   d. The multiplier is greater (less) than the multiplier in part a if $(b_1- b_2d_1/d_2)$ is greater (less) than zero. The multiplier is big if b_1 is big, b_2 is small, d_1 is small, and/or d_2 is big, *i.e.*, if investment is very sensitive to Y, investment is not very sensitive to i, money demand is not very sensitive to Y, money demand is very sensitive to i.

4. a. The IS curve shifts left. Output and the interest rate fall. The effect on investment is ambiguous because the output and interest rate effects work in opposite directions: the fall in output tends to reduce investment, but the fall in the interest rate tends to increase it.

   b. From 3c: $Y=[1/(1-c_1-b_1)]*[c_0-c_1T+ b_0-b_2i +G]$

   c. From the LM relation: $i= Y*d_1/d_2 – (M/P)/d_2$
   To obtain the equilibrium interest rate, substitute for Y from part b.

   d. $I= b_0+ b_1Y- b_2i= b_0+ b_1Y- b_2Y* d_1/d_2+ b_2(M/P)/d_2$
   To obtain equilibrium investment, substitute for Y from part b.

   e. Holding M/P constant, I increases with equilibrium output when $b_1>b_2 d_1/d_2$.
   Since a decrease in G reduces output, the condition under which a decrease in G increases investment is $b_1<b_2 d_1/d_2$.

f. The interpretation of the condition in part e is that the effect on I from Y has to be less than the effect from i after controlling for the endogenous response of i and Y, determined by the slope of the LM curve, d_1/d_2.

5. a. Y=C+I+G=200+.25*(Y-200)+150+.25Y-1000i+250
   Y=1100-2000i

   b. M/P=1600=2Y-8000i
   i=Y/4000-1/5

   c. Substituting b into a: Y=1000

   d. Substituting c into b: i=1/20=5%

   e. C=400; I=350; G=250; C+I+G=1000

   f. Y=1040; i=3%; C=410; I=380. A monetary expansion reduces the interest rate and increases output. The increase in output increases consumption. The increase in output and the fall in the interest rate increase investment.

   g. Y=1200; i=10%; C=450; I=350. A fiscal expansion increases output and the interest rate. The increase in output increases consumption.

   h. The condition from problem 3 is satisfied with equality (.25=1000*(2/8000)), so contractionary fiscal policy will have no effect on investment. When G=100: i=0%; Y=800; I=350; and C=350.

*6. a. The LM curve is flat
    b. Japan was experiencing a liquidity trap.
    c. Fiscal policy is more effective.

7. a. Increase G (or reduce T) and increase M.
   b. Reduce G (or increase T) and increase M. The interest rate falls. Investment increases, since the interest rate falls while output remains constant.

CHAPTER 6

1. a. False.
   b. False.
   c. False.
   d. False.
   e. True.
   f. False.
   g. Uncertain.
   h. True.
   i. False.

2. a. (Monthly hires+monthly separations)/monthly employment =6/93.8=6.4%

   b. 1.6/6.5=25%

   c. 2.4/6.5=37%. Duration is 1/.37 or 2.7 months.

   d. 4.9/57.3=9%.

   e. new workers: .35/4.9=7%; retirees: .2/4.9=4%.

3. a and b. Answers will depend on when the page is accessed.
   c. The decline in unemployment does not equal the increase in employment, because the labor force is not constant. It has increased over the period.

4. a. 66%; 66%*66%*66%= 29%; $(66\%)^6 = 8\%$

   b. $(66\%)^6 = 8\%$

   c. (for 1998): 875/6210= .14

5. a. Answers will vary.

   b and c. Most likely, the job you will have ten years later will pay a lot more than your reservation wage at the time (relative to your typical first job).

   d. The later job is more likely to require training and will probably be a much harder job to monitor. So, as efficiency wage theory suggests, your employer will be willing to pay a lot more than your reservation wage for the later job, to ensure low turnover and low shirking.

6. a. The computer network administrator has more bargaining power. She is much harder to replace.

6. b. The rate of unemployment is a key statistic. For example, when there are many unemployed workers it becomes easier for firms to find replacements. This reduces the bargaining power of workers.

7. a. $W/P=1/(1+\mu)=1/1.05=.95$

   b. Price setting: $u=1-W/P=5\%$

   c. $W/P=1/1.1=.91$; $u=1-.91=9\%$. The increase in the markup lowers the real wage. From the wage-setting equation, the unemployment rate must rise for the real wage to fall. So the natural rate increases.

CHAPTER 7

1. a. True.
    b. True.
    c. False.
    d. False.
    e. True.
    f. False.
    g. False.

2. a. IS right, AD right, AS up, LM up, Y same, i up, P up
    b. IS left, AD left, AS down, LM down, Y same, i down, P down

3. a.

	WS	PS	AS	AD	LM	IS	Y	i	P
Short run:	up	same	up	same	up	same	down	up	up
Medium run:	up	same	up	same	up	same	down	up	up

b.

	WS	PS	AS	AD	LM	IS	Y	i	P
Short run:	same	up	down	same	down	same	up	down	down
Medium run:	same	up	down	same	down	same	up	down	down

4. a. After an increase in the level of the money supply, output and the interest-rate eventually return to the same level. However, monetary policy is useful, because it can accelerate the return to the natural level of output.

    b. In the medium run, investment and the interest rate both change with fiscal policy.

    c. False. Labor market policies, such as unemployment insurance, can affect the natural level of output.

*5. a. Open answer. Firms may be so pessimistic about sales that they do not want to borrow at any interest rate.

    b. The IS curve is vertical; the interest rate does not affect equilibrium output.

    c. No change.

    d. The AD curve is vertical; the price level does not affect equilibrium output.

    e. The increase in z reduces the natural level of output and shifts the AS curve up. Since the AD curve is vertical, output does not change, but prices increase. Note that output is above its natural level.

    f. The AS curve shifts up forever, and prices keep increasing forever. Output does not change, and remains above its natural level forever.

176

6. a. The natural level of output is Y_n. Assuming that output starts at is natural level,
$P_0 = M_0 - (1/c)*Y_n$

b. Assuming that $P^e = P_0$: $Y = 2cM_0 - cP = 2cM_0 - cP_0 - cdY + cdY_n$
Recalling that $Y_n = c(M_0 - P_0)$: $Y = Y_n + (c/(1+c\ d))*M_0$

c. Investment goes up because output is higher and the interest rate is lower.

d. In the medium run, $Y = Y_n$

e. In the medium run, investment returns to its previous level, because output and the interest rate return to their previous levels.

CHAPTER 8

1. a. True.
   b. False.
   c. False.
   d. True.
   e. False.
   f. True.

2. a. No. In the 1970s, we experienced high inflation and high unemployment. The expectations-augmented Phillips curve is a relationship between inflation and unemployment conditional on the natural rate and inflation expectations. Given inflation expectations, increases in the natural rate (which result from adverse shocks to labor market institutions—increases in z—or from increases in the markup—which encompass oil shocks) lead to an increase in both the unemployment rate and the inflation rate. In addition, increases in inflation expectations imply higher inflation for any level of unemployment and tend to increase the unemployment rate in the short run (think of an increase in the expected price level, given last period's price, in the AD-AS framework). In the 1970s, both the natural rate and expected inflation increased, so both unemployment and inflation were relatively high.

   b. No. The expectations-augmented Phillips curve implies that maintaining a rate of unemployment below the natural rate requires increasing (not simply high) inflation. This is because inflation expectations continue to adjust to actual inflation.

3. a. $u_n = 0.1/2 = 5\%$

   b. $\pi_t = 0.1 - 2*.03 = 4\%$ every year beginning with year t.

   c. $\pi^e_t = 0$ and $\pi_t = 4\%$ forever. Inflation expectations will be forever wrong. This is unlikely.

   d. θ might increase because people's inflation expectations adapt to persistently positive inflation. The increase in θ has no effect on u_n.

   e. $\pi_5 = \pi_4 + .1 - .06 = 4\% + 4\% = 8\%$
   For $t > 5$, repeated substitution implies, $\pi_t = \pi_5 + (t-5)*4\%$.
   So, $\pi_{10} = 28\%$; $\pi_{15} = 48\%$.

   f. Inflation expectations will again be forever wrong. This is unlikely.

4. a. $\pi_t = \pi_{t-1} + 0.1 - 2u_t = \pi_{t-1} + 2\%$
   $\pi_t = 2\%$; $\pi_{t+1} = 4\%$; $\pi_{t+2} = 6\%$; $\pi_{t+3} = 8\%$.

   b. $\pi_t = 0.5\pi_t + 0.5\pi_{t-1} + 0.1 - 2u_t$
   or, $\pi_t = \pi_{t-1} + 4\%$

4. c. $\pi_t = 4\%$; $\pi_{t+1} = 8\%$; $\pi_{t+2} = 12\%$; $\pi_{t+3} = 16\%$

   d. As indexation increases, low unemployment leads to a larger increase in inflation over time.

5. a. A higher cost of production means a higher markup.

   b. $u_n = (0.08 + 0.1\mu)/2$; Thus, the natural rate of unemployment increases from 5% to 6% as μ increases from 20% to 40%.

6. a. Yes. The average rate of unemployment is down. In addition, the unemployment rate is at a historical low and inflation has not risen.

   b. The natural rate of unemployment has probably decreased.

7. An equation that seems to fit well is: $\pi_t - \pi_{t-1} = 6 - u_t$, which implies a natural rate of approximately 6%.

8. The relationships imply a lower natural rate in the more recent period.

CHAPTER 9

1. a. False.
   b. True.
   c. True.
   d. False.
   e. False.
   f. True.
   g. True.
   h. True.

2. a. The unemployment rate will increase by 1% per year when g=0.5%. Unemployment will increase unless the growth rate exceeds the sum of productivity growth and labor force growth.

   b. We need growth of 4.25% per year for each of the next four years.

   c. Okun's law is likely to become: $u_t - u_{t-1} = -0.4*(g_{yt} - 5\%)$

3. a. $u_n = 5\%$

   b. $g_{yt} = 3\%$; $g_{mt} = g_{yt} + \pi_t = 11\%$

   c.

	π	u	g_{yt}	g_{mt}
t-1:	8%	5%	3%	11%
t:	4%	9%	-7%	-3%
t+1:	4%	5%	13%	17%
t+2:	4%	5%	3%	7%

4. a. $\pi_t - \pi_{t-1} = -(u_t - .05)$
      $u_t - u_{t-1} = -.4*(g_{mt} - \pi_t - .03)$

   b. $\pi_t = 6.3\%$; $u_t = 8.7\%$
      $\pi_{t+1} = 1\%$; $u_{t+1} = 10.3\%$

   c. $u = 5\%$; $g_y = 3\%$; $\pi = -3\%$;

5. a. See text for full answer. Gradualism reduces need for large policy swings, with effects that are difficult to predict, but immediate reduction may be more credible and encourage rapid, favorable changes in inflation expectations. On the other hand, the staggering of wage decisions suggests that, if the policy is credible, a gradual disinflation is the option consistent with no change in the unemployment rate.

   b. Not clear, probably fast disinflation, depending on the features in c.

5. c. Some important features: the degree of indexation, the nature of the wage-setting process, and the initial rate of inflation.

*6. a. $u_n=K/2$; sacrifice ratio=.5

b. $\pi_t=10\%$; $\pi_{t+1}=8\%$; $\pi_{t+2}=6\%$; $\pi_{t+3}=4\%$; $\pi_{t+4}=2\%$

c. 5 years; sacrifice ratio=(5 point years of excess unemployment)/(10 percentage point reduction in inflation)=.5

d. $\pi_t=7.5\%$; $\pi_{t+1}=4.125\%$; $\pi_{t+2}=1.594\%$; 3 years of higher unemployment for a reduction of 10%: sacrifice ratio=0.3

e. $t+1$

f. Take measures to enhance credibility.

7. a. Inflation will start increasing.

b. It should let unemployment increase to its new, higher, natural rate.

Chapter 10

1. a. True.
   b. True.
   c. True.
   d. False.
   e. False.
   f. False.
   g. True.
   h. Uncertain.

2. a. Example: France: $(1.042)^{48}*5.150=\$37.1$ k.
   Germany: \$43.4 k; Japan: \$76.5 k; UK: \$22.5 k; U.S.: \$31.7 k

   b. 2.4

   c. yes.

3. a. \$5,000
   b. 2,500 pesos
   c. \$500
   d. \$1,000
   e. Mexican standard of living relative to the U.S.—exchange rate method: 1/10;
   PPP method: 1/5

4. a. $Y=63$
   b. Y doubles.
   c. Yes.
   d. $Y/N=(K/N)^{1/2}$
   e. $K/N=4$ implies $Y/N=2$. $K/N=8$ implies $Y/N=2.83$. Output less than doubles.
   f. No.
   g. No. In part f, we are looking at what happens to output when we increase capital only, not capital and labor in equal proportion. There are decreasing returns to capital.
   h. Yes.

5. The United States was making the most important technical advances. However, the other countries were able to make up much of their technological gap by importing the technologies developed in the United States, and hence, have higher technological progress.

6. Convergence for the France, Belgium, and Italy; no convergence for the second set of countries.

Chapter 11

1. a. Uncertain. True if saving includes public and private saving. False if saving only includes private saving.
   b. False.
   c. Uncertain.
   d. Uncertain.
   e. True.
   f. False.
   g. False.

2. a. No. (1) The Japanese rate of growth is not so high anymore. (2) If the Japanese saving rate has always been high, then this cannot explain the difference between the rate of growth in Japan and the US in the last 40 or 50 years. (3) If the Japanese saving rate has been higher than it used to be, then this can explain some of the high Japanese growth. The contribution of high saving to growth in Japan should, however, come to an end.

3. After a decade: higher growth rate. After five decades: growth rate back to normal, higher level of output per worker.

4. a. Higher saving. Higher output per worker
   b. Same output per worker. Higher output per capita.

5.* a. Yes.
   b. Yes.
   c. Yes.
   d. $Y/N = (K/N)^{1/3}$
   e. In steady state, $sf(K/N) = \delta K/N$, which, given the production function in part d, implies: $K/N=(s/\delta)^{3/2}$
   f. $Y/N =(s/\delta)^{1/2}$
   g. $Y/N = 2$
   h. $Y/N = 2^{1/2}$

6.* a. 1
   b. 1
   c. $K/N=.35$; $Y/N=.71$
   d. Using equation (11.3), the evolution of K/N is: 0.9, 0.82, 0.75

7. a. $K/N=(s/(2\delta))^2$; $Y/N=s/(4\delta)$
   b. $C/N=s(1-s)/(4\delta)$
   c-e. Y/N increases with s; C/N increases until s=.5, then decreases.

CHAPTER 12

1. a. True.
   b. False.
   c. True.
   d. False.
   e. True.
   f. False.
   g. True.
   h. Uncertain.
   i. False.

2. a. Lower growth in poorer countries. Higher growth in rich countries.
   b. Increase in R&D and in output growth.
   c. A decrease in the fertility of applied research; a (small) decrease in growth.
   d. A decrease in the appropriability of drug research. A drop in the development of new drugs. Lower technological progress and lower growth.

3. See discussion in section 12.2.

4. Examples will vary. Weakening patent protection would accelerate diffusion, but might also discourage R&D.

5. a. Year 1: 3000; Year 2: 3960
   b. Real GDP: 3300; output growth: 10%
   c. 20%
   d. Real GDP/Worker=30 in both years; productivity growth is zero.
   e. Real GDP: 3990; output growth: 33%.
   f. -0.8%
   g. Proper measurement implies real gdp/worker=36.3 in year 2. With improper measurement, productivity growth would be 21 percentage points lower and inflation 21% points higher.

6. a. Both lead to an initial decrease in growth
   b. Only the first leads to a permanent decrease in growth

7. a. $(K/(AN))^*=(s/(\delta+g_A+g_N))^2=1$; $(Y/(AN))^*=(1)^{1/2}$; $g_{Y/(AN)}=0$; $g_{Y/N}=4\%$; $g_Y=6\%$

   b. $(K/(AN))=(4/5)^2$; $(Y/(AN))^*=(4/5)$; $g_{Y/(AN)}=0$; $g_{Y/N}=8\%$; $g_Y=10\%$

   c. $(K/(AN))=(4/5)^2$; $(Y/(AN))^*=(4/5)$; $g_{Y/(AN)}=0$; $g_{Y/N}=4\%$; $g_Y=10\%$
   People are better off in case a. Given any set of initial values, the level of technology is the same in cases a and c, but the level of capital per effective worker is higher at every point in time in case a. Thus, since $Y/N=A*(Y/(AN))=A*(K/(AN))^{1/2}$, output per worker is always higher in case a.

8. There is a slowdown in growth and the rate of technological progress in the modern period. Japan's growth rate of technological progress is higher because it is catching up to the U.S. level of technology. Not all of the difference in growth rates of output per worker is attributable to the difference in rates of technological progress. A big part is attributable to the difference in rates of growth of capital per worker.

9.* a. Probably affects A. Think of climate.

b. Affects H.

c. Affects A. Strong protection tends to encourage more R&D but also to limit diffusion of technology.

d. May affect A through diffusion.

e. May affect K, H, and A. Lower tax rates increase the after-tax return on investment, and thus tend to lead to more accumulation of K and H and more R&D spending.

f. If we interpret K as private capital, than infrastructure affects A—*e.g.*, better transportation networks may make the economy more productive by reducing congestion time.

g. Assuming no technological progress, lower population growth implies higher steady-state level of output per worker. Lower population growth leads to higher capital per worker. If there is technological progress, there is no steady-state level of output per worker. In this case, however, lower population growth implies that output per worker will be higher at every point in time, for any given path of technology. See the answer to problem 7c.

Chapter 13

1. a. False.
   b. False.
   c. True.
   d. True.
   e. True.
   f. True.
   g. True.
   h. True.
   i. False.

2. a. $u=1-(1/(1+\mu))(A/A^e)$

   b. $u=1-(1/(1+\mu))=4.8\%$

   c. No. Since wages adjust to expected productivity, an increase in productivity eventually leads to equiproportional increases in the real wage implied by wage setting and price setting, at the original natural rate of unemployment. So equilibrium can be maintained without any change in the natural rate of unemployment.

3.* a. $P=P^e(1+\mu)(A^e/A)(Y/L)(1/A)$

   b. AS shifts down. Given $A^e/A=1$, an increase in A implies a fall in P, given Y. This occurs because for a given level of Y, unemployment is higher, so wages are lower and so, in turn, is the price level.

   c. There is now an additional effect, a fall in A^e/A. In effect, workers do not receive as much of an increase in wages as warranted by the increase in productivity. Compared to part b, nominal wages are lower, leading to a lower value of P given Y.

4. Discussion question.

5. a. Reduce the gap, if this leads to an increase in the relative supply of skilled workers.

   b. Reduce the gap, since it leads to a decrease in the relative supply of unskilled workers.

   c. Reduce the gap, since it leads to an increase in the relative supply of skilled workers.

   d. Increase the gap, if U.S. firms hire unskilled workers in Central America, since it reduces the relative demand for U.S. unskilled workers.

6. a. Textiles production is moving to low wage countries.

b. Possibly demographic changes, increased availability of child care outside the home, decline in labor supply for these positions.

c. Technological progress.

7. Discussion question.

CHAPTER 14

1. a. True.
    b. True.
    c. True.
    d. False.
    e. True.
    f. False.
    g. True.
    h. True. The nominal interest rate is always positive.
    i. False. The real interest rate can be negative.

2. a. Real. Nominal profits are likely to move with inflation; real profits are easier to forecast.
    b. Nominal. The payments are nominal.
    c. Nominal. If lease payments are in nominal terms, as is typical.

3. a. Exact: $r=(1+.04)/(1+.02)-1=1.96\%$; Approximation: $r=.04-.02=2\%$
    b. 3.60%; 4%
    c. 5.48%; 8%

4. a. No. Otherwise, nobody would hold bonds. Money would be more appealing: it pays at least a zero nominal interest rate and can be used for transactions.

    b. Yes. The real interest rate will be negative if expected inflation exceeds the nominal interest rate. Even so, the real interest rate on bonds (which pay nominal interest) will exceed the real interest rate on money (which does not pay nominal interest) by the nominal interest rate.

    c. A negative real interest rate makes borrowing very attractive, and leads to a large demand for investment.

5. a. The discount rate is the interest rate. So EPDV are (i) $2,000*(1-.25) under either interest rate and (ii) (1-.2)*$2,000 under either interest rate.

    b. The interest rate does not enter the calculation. Hence, you prefer ii to i since 20%<25%.

    Note that the answer to part a does not imply that saving will not accumulate. By retirement, the initial investment will have grown by a factor of $(1+i)^{40}$ in nominal terms and $(1+r)^{40}$ in real terms. As long as r is positive, the purchasing power of the initial investment will grow.

    In addition, this simple example omits an important real-world feature of retirement savings: the tax-free accrual of interest. As a result of this feature, the effective interest rate on retirement saving is much higher than the effective (after-tax) interest rate on ordinary saving.

6. a. $1000

b. Since the first payment occurs at the end of the year,
$V=\$z(1/1+i)(1-[1/(1+i)^{n-1}])/(1-[1/(1+i)])$.
10 years: $575.90; 20 years: $836.49; 30 years: $936.96; 60 years: $996.39

c. i=2%: consol $5000; 10 years: $816.22; 20 years: $1567.85; 30 years: $2184.44; 60 years: $3445.61

i=5%: consol $2000; 10 years: $710.78; 20 years: $1208.53; 30 years: $1514.11; 60 years: $1887.58

7. a. In the medium run, changes in inflation are reflected one for one in changes in the nominal interest rate. In other words, in the medium run, changes in inflation have no effect on the real interest rate.

b. Support.

c. The line should not go through the origin. The real interest rate is positive.

d. No. Even if monetary policy does not affect output or the real interest rate in the medium run, it can be used in the short run.

8.* a. The IS shifts right. At the same nominal interest rate, the real interest rate is lower, so output is higher.

b. The LM curve does not shift.

c. Output increases. The nominal interest rate is higher than in Figure 14-5. Whether the nominal interest rate is lower or higher than before the increase in money growth is ambiguous

d. Output is higher than in Figure 14-5. So, reasoning from the IS curve, the real interest rate must be lower. (In other words, while the nominal interest rate may increase relative to Figure 14-5, it increases by less than the increase in expected inflation. So the real interest rate decreases.)

CHAPTER 15

1. a. False.
   b. True.
   c. True.
   d. False.
   e. True.
   f. True.
   g. False.
   h. Uncertain/False.

2. a. $1+i=(\$F/\$P)^{1/n}$
   $i=(1000/800)^{1/3}-1=7.7\%$

   b. 5.7%

   c. 4.1%

3. The yield is approximately the average of the short term interest rates over the life of the bond.
   a. 5%.
   b. 5.25%
   c. 5.5%

4. Let r be the real interest rate, g the growth rate of dividends, and x be the risk premium. The price is given by:
   $1000/(1+r+x) + 1000(1+g)/(1+r+x)^2 + 1000(1+g)^2/(1+r+x)^3 \ldots$
   $=[1000/(1+r+x)][1 + (1+g)/(1+r+x) + (1+g)^2/(1+r+x)^2 + \ldots]=1,000/(r-g+x)$

   a. $50,000; $20,000
   b. $10,000; $7692.31
   c. $16,666.67; $11,111.11
   d. Increase. A fall in the risk premium is like a fall in the real interest rate.

5. a. Unexpected shift down of the LM curve. Unexpected fall in the interest rate and increase in Y. Stock prices increase.

   b. No change in stock prices.

   c. Ambiguous effect on stock prices. Unexpected expansionary fiscal policy means the interest rate is higher than expected (after the expected expansionary monetary policy) but so is output. The interest rate effect tends to reduce stock prices; the output effect to increase them.

6. a. See chapter.

6. b. Initially after the increase, the yield curve will slope down out to one-year maturities, then slope up. After one year, the yield curve will slope up. After three years, the yield curve will be flat.

7. At the start of the disinflation, markets expected that future interest rates would be lower, thus credible. During the rate cut in the recession, spreads went up, which implies that markets were expecting the anti-inflationary policy to continue with high short term interest rates after the inflation, as it did.

CHAPTER 16

1. a. False.
   b. True.
   c. False.
   d. False.
   e. False.
   f. True.
   g. True.

2. a. $.75*(1+1.05+1.05^2)*\$40,000=\$94,575$
   b. $\$194,575$
   c. $\$19,457.50$
   d. by $\$20,000/10=\$2,000$
   e. $.6*(1.05^2)*\$40,000*7/10=\$18,522$

3. EPDV is $\Pi/(r+\delta) = \$18,000/(r+0.08)$
   a. Buy. EPDV=$\$138,462>\$100,000$
   b. Break-even. EPDV=$\$100,000$
   c. Do not buy. EPDV=$\$78,260<\$100,000$

4. a. $\$44,000*(1-.4)*36-\$40,000*(1-.4)*38=\$38,400$
   b. $\$44,000*(1-.3)*36-\$40,000*(1-.3)*38=\$44,800$

5.* a. EPDV of future labor income = $30; consumption of $10 in all three periods.10,10,10
   b. young: -5; middle age: 15; old: -10
   c. -5+15-10=0
   d. $0 - 5N + 10N = 5N$
   e. young: 5; middle age: 12.5; old: 12.5; cannot borrow against future income when young.
   f. $0 + 12.5N - 2.5N = 0$
   g. $0 + 0 + 12.5N = 12.5N$
   h. Yes. By allowing people to have more even consumption, financial liberalization may lead t to less overall accumulation of capital.

6. On average, consumption is more than three times (3.4) bigger than investment. Relative to average changes, movements in consumption and investment are of the same magnitude, which implies investment is much more volatile than consumption. In 1991, the last recession year, the fall in consumption relative to its average was more than three times bigger than the fall in investment. This is consistent with the text's discussion (in Chapter 3) of the role of consumer confidence in this recession. On the other hand, over the years 1990-1992, the cumulative fall in investment relative to its average change was larger than the cumulative fall in consumption. In 1980 and 1982, the fall in investment relative to its average change was larger than the fall in consumption. Over the three years 1980-1982, the cumulative falls were similar, although a bit larger for investment. Investment actually increased in 1981. The changes in investment are consistent with the path of interest rates during the Volcker disinflation.

CHAPTER 17

1. a. True.
    b. False.
    c. False.
    d. True/Uncertain (They can rely on forecasts by others, but somebody has to do it.)
    e. False.
    f. True.
    g. False.

2. a. IS shifts right.

    b. The expected future real interest rate increases relative to the current real interest rate. IS shifts left.

    c. LM shifts right.

    d. The expected future real increase decreases. IS shifts right.

    e. Within the context of IS-LM, with a fixed capital stock, an increase in expected future taxes causes IS to shift left. However, the increase in future taxes (a deficit reduction program) will lead to lower real interest rates and increased investment in the medium run and higher output in the long run. The expected changes in the real interest rate and output tend to cause the IS curve to shift right. The net effect on the IS curve is ambiguous. Note that the model of the text has lump sum taxes. More generally, the tax increase may increase distortions in the economy. These effects tend to reduce output (or the growth rate).

    f. IS shifts left.

3. Rational expectations may be unrealistic, but it does not imply that every consumer has perfect knowledge of the economy. It implies that consumers use the best available information—models, data, and techniques—to assess the future and make decisions. Moreover, they do not have to work out the implications of economic models for the future by themselves; they can rely on the predictions of experts on television or in the newspapers. Essentially, rational expectations rules out systematic mistakes on the part of consumers. Thus, although rational expectations may not literally be true, it seems a reasonable benchmark for policy analysis.

4. These answers ignore any effect on capital accumulation and output in the long run.

    a. In the future, tax cuts will lead to a boom. This leads to higher expected output, lower expected taxes, but a higher expected interest rate in the future. The effect today on output is ambiguous.

    b. This means that the Fed will increase the interest rate in the future (shift LM left). The expected interest rate will increase more, but there is still the effect of lower expected taxes. The effect today on output is still ambiguous, more likely to be negative than in part a.

c. Future output will be higher, the future interest rate will not increase, and future taxes will be lower. So, output will go up today.

5. a and b. See the discussion in the text.

c. The gesture seemed to indicate that the Fed supported deficit reduction, and would be willing to conduct expansionary monetary policy in the future to offset the direct negative effects on output from spending cuts and tax increases. A belief that the Fed would be willing to act in this way would tend to increase expected future output (relative to the case where the Fed did nothing) and reduce expected future interest rates. Both of these effects tend to increase output in the short-run.

6. a. The yield curve got flatter between November 1992 and August 1993, with very little change in short-term interest rates. This suggests that the expected future short-term interest rate fell, i.e., that the Fed was expected to adopt a more expansionary stance.

b. No recession after 1993. This is consistent with expectations that the Fed would support the deficit reduction with relatively expansionary policy.

c. Yes.

d. Higher growth rates in the 1990s increased tax revenues and reduced transfer payments.

Chapter 18

1. a. True.
   b. False.
   c. False.
   d. False.
   e. True.
   f. False.

2. The franc steadily depreciated against the DM from 1979 to 187, was then steady with little volatility from 1988 to 1991, and was more or less steady with some volatility from 1992 to 1998.

3. <u>Domestic Country Balance of Payments</u> ($)

   Current Account

Exports	25	
Imports	145 (=100+45)	
Trade Balance		-120 (=25-145)
Investment Income Received	0	
Investment Income Paid	15	
Net Investment Income		-15 (=0-15)
Net Transfers Received		-25
Current Account Balance		-160 (=-120-15-25)

   Capital Account

Increase in Foreign Holdings of U.S. Assets	80 (=65+15)	
Increase in U.S. Holdings of Foreign Assets	-50	
Net Increase in Foreign Holdings		130 (=80-(-50))
Statistical Discrepancy		30 (=160-130 or =35-5)

3.(cont) <u>Foreign Country Balance of Payments</u> ($)

Current Account

Exports	145	
Imports	25	
Trade Balance		120
Investment Income Received	15	
Investment Income Paid	0	
Net Investment Income		15
Net Transfers Received		25
Current Account Balance		160

Capital Account

Increase in Foreign Holdings	-50	
Increase in Domestic Holdings	80	
Net Increase in Foreign Holdings		-130
Statistical Discrepancy		-30

4. Current account deficits look bad. Net capital inflows look good. We know from balance of payments accounting, however, that we cannot have one without the other. The evidence does not support either argument. Contrary to what the Democrats said, the trade deficit was due to a large output expansion in the United States, which lead to a large increase in imports (see the In Depth Box in Chapter 20), not primarily to a loss of competitiveness. Contrary to what the President said, the large net capital inflows were needed to finance the trade deficit; they were not a sign that foreign investors were eager to invest in the United States.

5. a. The nominal return on the U.S. bond is $10,000/(9615.38) - 1 = 4\%$.
The nominal return on the German bond is 5%.

b. Uncovered interest parity implies that the dollar is expected to appreciate by 1%. Thus, the expected exchange rate is $.99*(.95)=0.9405$ $/DM.

c. If you expect the dollar to depreciate instead, purchase the German bond as you expect the return (in $) to be more than 5%.

d. The German currency depreciates by 5.26%, so the total return on the German bond (in $) is $5-5.26= -0.26\%$. Investing in the U.S. bond would have produced a sure 4% return.

e. The uncovered interest parity condition is about equality of expected returns, not equality of actual returns.

6. a. Simply substitute F for E^e in the derivation of uncovered interest parity in the text. We no longer need to use E^e as the price of foreign exchange will be fixed when we liquidate our position in German bonds and move funds back to the United States.

b. The forward rate consistent with covered interest parity is the same as the expected exchange rate consistent with uncovered interest parity.

c. Go long or short in U.S. bonds, depending on the forward exchange rate.

d. Surprises in the exchange rate no longer affect actual returns on your investment.

Chapter 19

1. a. False.
   b. Uncertain.
   c. False.
   d. False.
   e. True.
   f. True.

2. a. $\varepsilon=EP^*/P$. Apply proposition 8 to $(EP^*)/P$ and then proposition 7 to (EP^*).

   b. If $\Delta P/P > \Delta P^*/P^*$ and $\Delta E/E = 0$, then $\Delta\varepsilon/\varepsilon <0$, so the real exchange rate is decreasing (the domestic currency is appreciating) over time. Given the Marshall-Lerner condition, this implies net exports are falling.

   The price of domestic goods is rising faster than the price of foreign goods, while the exchange rate is constant. As domestic goods are becoming more expensive than foreign goods, consumers in both countries shift their purchases away from goods in the high-inflation country to the low-inflation one.

3. a. $Y=C+I+G+X-Q=20+0.8^*(y-10)+G+0.3Y^*-0.3Y$
   $Y=24+2G+0.6Y^*$
   $Y=44+0.6Y^*$

   The multiplier is 2 ($=1/(1-.8+.3)$) when foreign output is fixed. The closed economy multiplier is 5 ($=1/.5$). It differs from the open economy multiplier because, in the open economy, only some of the demand falls on domestic goods.

   b. Since the countries are identical, $Y=Y^*=110$. Taking into account the endogeneity of foreign income, the multiplier equals $(1-0.8 -0.3^*0.6 +0.3)^{-1}=3.125$. The multiplier is higher than the open economy multiplier above because it takes into account the impact of higher imports on foreign income, which raises exports.

   c. If $Y=125$, then foreign output $Y^*=44+0.6^*91225)=119$. Using these two facts and the equation $Y=24+2G+0.6Y^*$ yields: $125=24+2G+0.6^*(119)$. Solving for G gives $G=14.8$. In the domestic country, $NX=0.3^*(119)-0.3^*(125)=-1.8$; $T-G=10-14.8=-4.8$. In the foreign country, $NX^*=1.8$; $T^*-G^*=0$.

   d. If $Y=Y^*=125$, then we have: $125=24+2G+0.6^*(125)$, which implies $G=G^*=13$. In both countries, net exports are still zero, but the budget deficit has increased by 3.

   e. In part, fiscal coordination is difficult to achieve because of the benefits of doing nothing, as indicated from part c.

4. a. A tax on foreign goods of rate τ affects the price paid for imports. Instead of ε, it is now equal to $(1+\tau)\varepsilon$. Imports are given by $Q((1+\tau)\varepsilon, Y)$. The price of exports is unaffected, so exports are still given by $X(\varepsilon, Y^*)$.

b. The higher price of foreign goods to domestic consumers reduces imports (but does not affect demand for exports), which given domestic income increases NX. This shifts the IS curve to the right, increasing domestic equilibrium income. Higher domestic income offsets some of the initial increase in NX, but the overall effect is still favorable.

c. The tax has opposite effects in the foreign country, affecting their exports negatively, shifting the IS curve to the left, which reduces equilibrium income.

d. Each shift in the IS curve will be reversed, but the overall volume of trade, described by $Q+Q^*$ will fall. If agents simply substitute domestic goods for foreign goods, output will remain the same.

5. a. The share of Japanese spending relative to U.S. GDP is 1%.
   b. The impact on U.S. GDP is 0.1%.
   c. The impact on U.S. GDP is 1%.
   d. This is an overstatement. The numbers above indicated that even if U.S. exports fall by 5%, the effect is to reduce growth by 1%. This is small relative to GDP, but large relative to normal growth (of around 3%).

6. a. Initially, net exports and output fall.
   b. After six months, net exports and output increase.

Chapter 20

1. a. Uncertain.
    b. False/uncertain.
    c. True.
    d. True.
    e. False.
    f. False.

2. a. Before the devaluation, the fixed exchange rate is credible, so the interest rate is simply the foreign interest rate. After the devaluation, the fixed exchange rate is again credible, so the interest rate will not change. The devaluation increases net exports by the Marshall-Lerner condition and increases output.

    b. The domestic interest rate must rise above the foreign rate. Output may not increase as the effects of the devaluation may be offset by the effect of a higher interest rate.

3. a. Monetary policy is ineffective in the Follower countries. The fixed exchange rate implies that the domestic interest rate is fixed, given the Leader interest rate.

    b. It is true that the Leader country's exchange rate is essentially fixed, but it still operates as if it were in a flexible exchange rate regime. The leader country is free to change interest rates as it wishes, since the fixed exchange rate is not its target. In other words, monetary policy is effective for the Leader country.

    c. Follower countries must increase interest rates as well. This leads to a contraction in output. If Follower countries did nothing, their currencies would depreciate.

4. a. IS shifts left, because domestic exports fall given any exchange rate (and hence any value of the interest rate). Output falls.

    b. E increases, given any value of the home interest rate, so IS shifts right. The interest parity line also shifts right. As a result, E increases, NX increases, and Y increases. The home interest rate also increases, but by less than the foreign interest rate.

    c. The effects of a monetary contraction abroad on home output are ambiguous. A monetary contraction abroad reduces foreign output and increases the foreign interest rate. The output effect tends to reduce home output (because home exports tend to fall). The interest rate tends to increase home output (because the home currency depreciates, which has a positive effect on home NX).

5. The question should refer to an economy with flexible exchange rates. In this case, the proper policy combines expansionary policy (which leads to depreciation, but to an increase in output) with contractionary fiscal policy (which offsets the increase in output from monetary policy).

6. Consumption and investment both increase. The effect on net exports is ambiguous: higher output leads to lower net exports, but depreciation leads to higher net exports.

Chapter 21

1. a. Uncertain (the problem was not the return but the parity chosen)
   b. True.
   c. Uncertain.
   d. True/uncertain.
   e. False.

2. a. Causes a real depreciation, which leads to an increase in demand and output.

   b. Causes a decrease in the real interest rate, which leads to an increase in demand and output.

   c. First, unequal inflation rates lead to effects on the real exchange rate. If inflation is high (and of similar magnitude) at home and abroad, then there is little effect on the real exchange rate, and the effect in part a goes away. Second, in the medium run, inflation has no effect on the real interest rate, so the effect in part b goes away.

3. a. In the short run, output increases, the real exchange rate does not change, and the nominal interest rate does not change (it remains equal to the world interest rate under fixed exchange rates. In the medium run, output returns to its natural level, the real exchange rate appreciates, and the nominal interest rate remains unchanged.

   b. In the short run, consumption and investment increase, but net exports fall. In the medium run, the consumption and investment returns to their original levels, since output returns to its natural level and the interest rate is unchanged. Net exports fall by an amount equal to the increase in government spending.

   c. Budget deficits do lead to trade deficits, but not mechanically. Changes in the budget deficit lead to changes in output and the real exchange rate, both of which affect the trade deficit directly.

4. a. Reunification implies an excessive appreciation of the East German currency. It leads to a recession.

   b. Output remains low until prices have decreased enough relative to West German prices so as to reestablish the right real exchange rate.

   c. Prices must fall. If there is no productivity growth, nominal wages must fall.

5. An increase in the perceived probability of devaluation makes Brazilian stocks much less attractive than non-Brazilian stocks. Financial investors sell off their holdings and stock prices fall. They fall until the expected return in Reals is large enough to compensate for the expected devaluation of the Real. After the devaluation, however, if investors do not expect further devaluations (any more than they did before the crisis), it is reasonable for stock prices to recover so sharply.

Chapter 21: Appendix

1. Step 1
   Using the two interest rate relations: $(1+r_t)=(1+r^*_t)[E^e_{t+1}(1+\pi^{*e}_t)/(E_t(1+\pi^e_t))]$

   Step 2
   From the definition of inflation, $(1+\pi^e_t)=P^e_{t+1}/P_t$

   And similarly, $(1+\pi^{*e}_t)=P^{*e}_{t+1}/P^*_t$

   Using these two relations in the term in brackets (in Step 1) gives:

$$[E^e_{t+1}(1+\pi^{*e}_t)/(E_t(1+\pi^e_t))]= [E^e_{t+1}(P^{*e}_{t+1}/P^*_t)/(E_t(P^e_{t+1}/P_t))]= [E^e_{t+1}(P^{*e}_{t+1}/P^e_{t+1})/(E_t(P^*_t/P_t))]$$
$$= \varepsilon^e_{t+1}/\varepsilon_t$$

   where the second equality follows from reorganizing terms, and the third follows from the definition of the real exchange rate.

   Replacing in the previous equation gives equation (21.A1):

$$(1+r_t)=(1+r^*_t)[\ \varepsilon^e_{t+1}/\varepsilon_t]$$

2. a. 4%=3%+x so x=1% expected real depreciation each year.

   b. 10%=6%+x so x=4% expected nominal depreciation of the currency each year.

   c. You would purchase the domestic bond because the foreign bond will only yield 6% and there is a loss on your position in the foreign currency.

Chapter 22

1. a. False.
    b. True.
    c. Uncertain.
    d. False.
    e. True.

2. a. Draw the IS and LM curves so they cross close to i=1. Note, however, that the LM curve cannot cross the horizontal axis.

    b. No. It cannot decrease the current interest rate below zero.

    c. If the expected nominal interest rate was positive in the first place, then the Central Bank can announce that it will decrease it. Then, the expected real interest rate will decrease, the IS curve will shift to the right, and output will increase.

    d. Open.

3. a. Short-term unemployment has more effect. The long-term may not be searching and may not be very employable.

    b. $u=0.1/[(1.1)(1-0.5\beta)]$

    c. If $\beta=0$, 0.4, 0.8, the natural rate $=9.1\%$, 11.4%, 15.2%.

4. a. Higher unemployment implies lower wages given expected prices. This implies lower prices given expected prices. Equivalently, it implies lower inflation given expected inflation, which here equals past inflation.

    b. $\pi - \pi_{t-1} = (\mu+z) - \alpha u_S$

    or equivalently: $\pi - \pi_{t-1} = (\mu+z) - \alpha(u-u_L)$

    c. The curve will shift to the right. More overall unemployment is needed to achieve the same decrease in inflation.

    d. Yes. If disinflation leads to an increase in u_L, disinflation will be less than predicted by the standard relation.

5. Open, but although the effect on overall unemployment is indeed as stated, one must worry about what happens to the workers who become unemployed. If they cannot insure themselves against unemployment, the state has a role to play.

Chapter 23

1. a. True.
    b. False.
    c. False.
    d. False.
    e. False.
    f. False.

2. a. If money growth = 25%, 50%, 75%, seignorage=162.5, 325, 487.5

    b. In the medium run, if money growth = 25%, 50%, 75%, seignorage=162.5, 200, 112.5

    c. max $(0.9-\Delta M/M)(\Delta M/M)$ implies $\Delta M/M = 45\%$

3. a. Would decrease the effect of inflation on real tax revenues.

    b. Would decrease the effect of inflation on real tax revenues.

    c. Would decrease the effect of inflation on real tax revenues, but would also have other effects. The income tax can tax the rich at a higher rate than the poor, but the sales tax rate is the same for rich and poor.

4. The end to the crisis depends on shifting the composition of taxes. Workers are already paying an inflation tax.

    The central bank must make a credible commitment that it will no longer automatically monetize the government debt. Although a currency board would do this, it is a drastic and perhaps unnecessary step.

    Price controls may help, but price controls without other policy changes only cause distortions and are a recipe for failure.

    A recession is not needed, but it may happen. Although nominal rigidities are less important during hyperinflations—which implies that the sacrifice ratio is small—the issue of credibility remains. Unless firms and workers believe in the stabilization program, a severe recession may be the result.

Chapter 24

1. a. False.
   b. Uncertain.
   c. False.
   d. False.
   e. Uncertain.

2. a. True/Uncertain.
   b. False.
   c. False.
   d. Uncertain.

3. a. 35 years.
   b. 70 years.
   c. Open, but one can easily think of much faster catching up.

4. a. E^e and i^* enter because they affect E, which affects net exports.

   b. See Chapter 20.

   c. In panel (a), the IS curve shifts to the right: a higher E^e means a higher E, higher exports, and and higher demand. In panel (b), the relation between the interest rate and the exchange rate shifts to the right: E increases for a given interest rate.

   d. Output goes up and the exchange rate increases (depreciates).

   e. To maintain the parity, the central bank must increase the interest rate by reducing the money supply. This causes the LM curve to shift left. Despite the shift of the IS curve (part c), output falls. At the initial level of output, an unchanged exchange rate would imply no change in net exports. However, the interest rate would be higher, so investment would fall, which is inconsistent with an unchanged level of output.

   f. One way is to rewrite C(Y-T) as C(Y-T,E) with an increase in E decreasing consumption.

   g. Output may go down. The depreciation increases net exports, but decreases domestic demand.

Chapter 25

1. a. False.
   b. True/Uncertain.
   c. False.
   d. False.
   e. Uncertain.

2. Answers will vary.

3. a. If you think that voters care a lot about current conditions, you may want to come into the elections with low inflation and low unemployment. So, you may want to have higher unemployment early on, to decrease inflation, and unemployment lower than the natural rate the year before the election.

   b. If voters have rational expectations, they will understand what you are trying to do. You will not be able to affect the unemployment rate. You are better off keeping inflation constant, and unemployment at the natural rate.

4. Answers will vary.

5. a. 1/2 times the expected rate of inflation if the Democrats win plus 1/2 times the expected rate of inflation if the Republicans win.

   b. Low unemployment, high inflation ($\pi > \pi^e$)

   c. High unemployment, low inflation ($\pi < \pi^e$)

   d. Yes, if one looks at the first two years of each administration, not just the first.

   e. Unemployment equal to the natural rate, high inflation. This is because expected inflation is very high, so $\pi = \pi^e$.

6. a. If the Republicans cut military spending, the Democrats get 1 if they cut welfare, but 3 if they do not. So they will not cut welfare. The Republicans will get –2.

   b. If the Republicans do not cut military spending, the Democrats get –2 if they cut welfare, but only –1 if they do not. So they will not cut welfare. The Republicans will get –1.

   c. Given the answers above, the Republicans do better when they do not cut military spending, so they will not cut. The Democrats will not cut either. The two parties are locked in a bad equilibrium. They could make a deal: both vote for cuts. If they do, they will both be better off.

Chapter 26

1. a. False.
   b. False/Uncertain.
   c. False.
   d. False/Uncertain.
   e. False.
   f. True/Uncertain.

2. a. Demand for M1 falls while demand for M2 is unchanged. People shift funds from savings accounts to time deposits.

   b. Demand for M1 increases as people transfer funds from money market funds to checking accounts. Demand for M2 remains unchanged.

   c. Shift in the composition of M1 (and consequently M2) as people hold more currency and make fewer trips to the bank while holding smaller checking account balances.

   d. The demand for M2 increases as the benefit of holding government securities falls.

3. a. 4%-0%=4%; 14%-10%=4%

   b. 4% * (1-0.25)-0%=3%; 14% * (1-0.25)-10%=10.5%-10%=0.5%

   c. Yes, given the deductibility of nominal mortgage interest payments in the United States.

4. Probably not. These two facts suggest that there has been a shift between M2 and M1, and the demand for money has shifted.

5. Increase in H through open market operations or lending through the discount window. Decrease in θ, reserve requirements. Decrease in c, the proportion of currency kept by people—by making checking accounts more attractive.

6. In principle, yes. Investment tax credits, which give tax breaks to firms that invest, can help increase investment. However, fiscal policy is probably less flexible than monetary policy in this context.

Chapter 27

1. a. True.
   b. False.
   c. Uncertain.
   d. False.
   e. False.

2. a. Interest payments are 10% of GDP, so the primary surplus is 10%-4%=6%.

   b. Real interest payments are (10%-7%)*100%=3% of GDP. So the inflation adjusted surplus is 6%-3%=3%.

   c. Unemployment is higher by 2%. By Okun's law (with a normal growth rate of 3%), output is lower by 2%. Using the rule of thumb in the text, the surplus is lower by 0.5*2%=1%. So the cyclically adjusted, inflation adjusted surplus is 2%.

   d. The change in the debt to GDP ratio = (3%-2%)*100% - 3% = -2%. The debt to GDP ratio falls by 2% a year.

   e. In 10 years, the debt to GDP ratio will be about 80%.

3. a. The new interest rate is 10%+0.5*20%=20%. So assuming that expected depreciation was previously zero, the domestic interest rate increases from 10% to 20%.

   b. The real interest rate increases from 3% to 13%. The high real interest rate is likely to decrease growth.

   c. The official deficit increases from 4% to 14% of GDP. The inflation adjusted deficit increases from –3% (a surplus) to 7% (a deficit).

   d. The change in the debt ratio = (13%-(-2%))*100%-3%=12%. It goes up very quickly.

   e. Self-fulfilling worries.

4. First, even a temporary deficit leads to an increase in the national debt, and therefore to higher interest payments. This, in turn, implies continued deficits, higher taxes, or lower government spending in the future. Second, the evidence does not support the Ricardian equivalence proposition. Third, if Ricardian equivalence did hold, then a deficit would not stimulate the economy. Fourth, war-time economies are already low-unemployment economies. There is no need for further stimulation by using deficits rather than tax finance. The only correct part of the statement is the first sentence. A deficit can be preferable to higher taxes during a war, but not for the reasons stated here.

5. Discussion question. Also see the box on Social Security in Chapter 11 (p. 215).